D1595431

MILITARY MEMOIRS

Edited by

Brigadier Peter Young

D.S.O., M.C., M.A., F.S.A., F.R.HIST.S., F.R.G.S.

Roger de Mauni, 1871

MILITARY MEMOIRS

Roger de Mauni

The Franco-Prussian War

Edited by

DAVID CLARKE

LONGMAN

LONGMAN GROUP LIMITED
London

*Associated companies, branches and
representatives throughout the world*

© *Longman Group Ltd 1970*

First published 1970

ISBN O 582 12719 X

*Printed in Great Britain by
W & J Mackay & Co Ltd, Chatham*

Contents

The maps are by John Flower

Note on the Series

by PETER YOUNG

In planning a series of this sort, there is a bewildering variety of factors to be considered. Of these perhaps the chief is the fundamental question: 'Why do people read Military History?' Is it because the truth is more attractive than fiction? Baron de Marbot, although his tales had unquestionably improved in the telling, has an interest which Brigadier Gerard, despite the narrative skill of Conan Doyle, cannot rival. Marbot's memory could play him false in matters of detail, but not as to the sense of period. He brings to life the atmosphere of the Grand Army in which he served. Marbot, regrettably, is too well known, both in French and English, to parade with the veterans of this series. We have endeavoured to present memoirists who for one reason or another are relatively unknown to the English-speaking public.

In modern times, memoir writing seems to have become the prerogative of generals. One is not, however, without hopes of finding a voice or two from the ranks to conjure up the fields of Flanders or the deserts of North Africa. Of course, we have not rejected generals altogether. But on the whole we have tried to rescue 'old swordsmen' from oblivion. The fighting soldier is more attractive than an officer with a distinguished series of staff appointments to his credit; the tented field has an appeal which the dull round of garrison life cannot rival. We have also avoided those veterans who, their Napier at their elbow, submerge their personal recollections in a mass of ill-digested second-hand campaign history. These are the most maddening of all. What details they could have given us had they chosen to!

The trouble is that memoirists take so much for granted. They assume that we know all about the military organization and tactics of their day. And so we must just be thankful for small mercies. You will not get a fight on every page, but gradually a picture is built up. One comes to visualize the manners of a bygone age, to see how people then could endure the privations of a campaign, the rough surgery of the battlefield, or the administrative neglect of their commanders. In the end we come almost to speak their language, and to hear them speak.

Introduction

In the summer of 1871 a well-known English divine, Charles James Vaughan, Master of the Temple and one-time headmaster of Harrow, was holidaying on the south coast at Folkestone. There he met a noble French family, the Baron et Baronne de M., their daughter Louise, and their son who had lately rejoined them from France. The family had taken refuge in England after the fall of the Second Empire in the early part of the Franco-Prussian War. Their son, Roger, had remained behind to serve for eight months in the Gardes Mobiles, or reserve French forces. He had kept a diary of his experiences, which was now being published in Paris.

C. J. Vaughan, who was always interested in the young, was fascinated by the diary. 'It cannot be without interest', he wrote, 'for those who would look below the surface of history, to study those personal incidents of which statesmen and tacticians keep no record. It is well that the distant glitter of arms and camps should sometimes be exchanged for a nearer and more microscopic view of the privations and miseries by which defeats and victories alike are purchased. Every new glimpse of the realities of warfare is a new motive for an earnest and even jealous maintenance of God's highest blessing of peace'. He persuaded the family to allow him to arrange for an English edition to which he dedicated a Preface from which the above passage is quoted.

The diary duly appeared in 1872, published by Strahan and Co. of Ludgate Hill, with the title *Eight Months on Duty: the Diary of a Young Officer in Chanzy's Army*. Vaughan had no part in the translation. 'The hands that have accomplished it', he noted cryptically, 'are the best guarantee for its fidelity and its beauty.' It is this translation that I have used, as it seems to me to have the proper flavour of the epoch. I have slightly rearranged the text in some places, and have incorporated into the main body some letters which in the original were in an appendix at the end, but otherwise it is as Vaughan, and presumably Roger de Mauni, originally approved it.

In neither the English edition nor in the first French edition is the author's name given in full, nor the name of his family. After the lapse of nearly one hundred years it was not easy to penetrate this

ix

anonymity. The first clear evidence of his identity which I obtained was from the regimental lists still held in the Mairie at Mortain in Normandy, which give the name of a certain Roger de Mauni, a native of Bourg Achard in the Eure, who, living in Paris in 1870, was called to the colours with the Garde Mobile of the Seine and later gazetted in the battalion of Mortain in the Régiment de la Manche. Much searching would have been avoided if I had had access to the second French Edition of the diary, a copy of which has now come into my possession. For this, though published in 1872 only some months after the original, gives the author's full name. In it he explains that his previous reticence was the result of an army order that forbade the discussion of military matter in print on a personal basis, but that now that he had fully reverted to being a private citizen he felt that he could ignore this constraint. He also appended to the diary a history of the events which surrounded it, much as I have done for the purpose of this edition, though I note that our views on certain personalities are widely different. Gambetta was for Roger de Mauni the prime architect of military misfortune and d'Aurelle de Paladines a general far superior to Chanzy—I doubt whether history would really support this view.

For the loan of this second edition and for almost everything else I know about Roger de Mauni I am deeply indebted to Monsieur Amaury de Riencourt, who has supplied me with a wealth of personal and other information.

Roger de Mauni was born at St Germain-en-Laye in 1847. His father was a Cuirassier officer who had retired in 1830; through him Roger was descended from ancestors who had served as King's musketeers, and through his mother he was related to Napoleon I's Marshal Macdonald. Prevented by his health from following a military career, he was himself, at the age of twenty-three, in the process of entering the diplomatic service with a distinguished academic record when war broke out in 1870. Disenchanted as he must have been with the military capacity of his native country, he returned to Normandy after the war as a private citizen and devoted most of his time to scientific studies and experiments. These were financially unrewarding, for in 1885 he went bankrupt. His sister Louise came to his rescue and paid his debts. For this kindness he never really forgave her, and their friendship, so clearly depicted in the letters he had written her during the war, came to an end. They never spoke to each other again. Louise, however, was a remarkable woman. She married the Marquis de Riencourt and a year after his death, in 1899, emigrated with her only son to Athens, where they both became Greek citizens.

Louise had had a lifelong passion for Greece and she became a power in the political life of that country; indeed, it was partly her influence on her great friend Venezelos that was instrumental in triggering the disastrous Greco-Turkish War of the early 1920s. Her son Raoul, the present Marquis de Riencourt who still lives in Paris, returned to France in 1906. Louise remained in Greece. She was destined never to return to France; she died in Athens at the age of ninety-six in 1941, two weeks before the Germans entered the city.

Meanwhile Roger too had married, Valentine Lemercier de Nerville, and at about the turn of the century had acquired a country house in the shape of the Château de Bosgouet, a charming property some three kilometres outside Bourg Achard. He had also returned to writing, and under the pen-name of Félix Depardieu he produced scientific tracts such as *The Rights and Responsibilities of Inventors of Machines of War* (1892) and *Pneumatic Bindings and Resistance to Movement* (1899). He also produced three novels: *Anna* (1899), *Trop Jeune* (1900) and *La fille d'Aglaure* (1901). Félix Depardieu was also to enter into print locally with decided views on the Dreyfus affair, but his most sensational literary effort appeared in 1912. This took the form of a supposed report to King Emmanuel III of Italy from a military attaché serving with the French forces in the course of a decisive battle during an imaginary war between France and Germany. The supposed date of the dispatch was June 1915. In the war-anxious climate of 1912 the booklet raised a degree of interest and ran to more than one edition. In brief, the theme was that France and Germany were once again, as in 1870, sole antagonists (Britain, Italy and Austria remaining neutral). It was assumed that Germany had respected the neutrality of Belgium (in this Roger de Mauni gave too much honour to the German side) and had therefore invaded French soil in the direction of Nancy. Part of the intention of the work was to draw attention to the weakness of the French defences in this region, for Nancy was a town whose fortification had been forbidden secretly under the terms of the Peace of Frankfort at the end of the Franco-Prussian War. The point made was that the French had awoken to this danger and by fortifying Nancy were able to stem the German advances and to bring the invading armies to decisive battle on the great plain of the Voivre. As a result the German forces were completely defeated and France regained those territories of Alsace and

Lorraine that she had lost in 1871. The imaginary campaign involved considerable use of air power both on the battlefield and as a threat to major cities.

It was a lively and prescient work which gained even wider recognition when in 1915 the French and German Armies were in actual fact locked in combat on the Voivre; the coincidence of place and date could not fail to be noticed. So it was that when in that year another work in the same format appeared from the pen of Félix Depardieu, it was given a certain amount of attention. This time it was a Swiss Colonel giving to the Swiss President his appreciation of the war, but this time of the real war and at the real date of 1915. At this moment Roger de Mauni, alias Félix Depardieu, alias Colonel Hubert de Payerne, concluded that on balance Germany had lost and that her best course was to sue for peace and to be prepared to foot the bill. It was to be a long time before this conclusion was to catch up with reality.

By this time too Roger was again in uniform. On the outbreak of war he had importuned the military authorities to give him an active post, having been passed medically fit despite his age of sixty-seven. He was denied his wish to be sent to the Front; instead, he joined the Staff of the military college of St Cyr and devoted his considerable abilities to instructing officer cadets. After the armistice he returned to Bosgouet and took up once more his interest in 'pneumatic coverings for vehicle wheels'. The unsuccessful outcome of his scientific studies was always a disappointment; however, there was not much time left to him. Shortly after 1919 he became ill and on 17 May 1921 he died. In accordance with his own wishes he was buried at Bosgouet in the uniform of a Captain of the French Army, which, says his obituary, the military authorities surely ought to have decorated with the cross of the Légion d'Honneur, for had he not served with distinction in two of France's wars? His wife (they had no children) lived on in increasingly difficult financial circumstances until she too was laid to rest in the same place in 1953 at the age of ninety-two, one of the few women who could compare the exodus of 1940 with that of 1870, for she had lived through both.

Jean de Rougé, the son of Fernand de Rougé of the diary, became during Roger's lifetime a close friend of the de Riencourt family. He often referred to the visits of Roger de Mauni to his father and how struck they were by the remarkable eccentricity of that gifted man; just as the townspeople used to find something mildly astonishing in the sight of that military figure, dressed in brown velvet coat and baggy trousers of the same material, mounted on a tricycle pedalling through the streets of Rouen.

Bosgouet is now a children's holiday home and has lost all trace of its one-time owners. But the churchyard remembers them. There is a polished marble tomb on which the inscription reads:

Ci-Gît Noble Homme Roger Alfred GRATIEN

dernier Baron de Mauni

et sa femme

Valentine Lemercier de Nerville

Priez pour Eux

Acknowledgements

I should like to acknowledge my thanks first and foremost to the Marquis de Riencourt and to Monsieur Amaury de Riencourt. The latter is the great-nephew and godson of Roger de Mauni, and himself author in English of such works of distinction as *The Roof of the World* and *The Soul of India*. By his kindness in the loan of photographs and of historical material it has been possible to form some idea of the life and character of the author of this diary.

I am particularly grateful, too, to Colonel John Davis, 7th Gurkha Rifles, who being at the Ecole de Guerre at the time of my investigations, so kindly followed leads and visited the Château of Bosgouet and as a result of his conversation with M. Lethellier, the Deputy Mayor, produced the clues which led finally to the de Riencourt family.

I am also most grateful to the various members of the de Mauny family who, themselves originating from Normandy, gave me much help in investigating the possibility of some connection between their own family and Roger de Mauni.

I should like to express my thanks to Colonel Annequin and to the Services Historiques de l'Armée for their investigations into the archives, to the officials of Mortain and other Norman towns who so kindly answered my letters and produced much useful information. I should also like to thank Colonel Gérard de Lassus for his continuing interest and help in my reserches into the Franco-Prussian War and to Father E. A. Janneau of Shaftesbury for his genealogical researches.

Mr Sussams, Borough Librarian of Folkestone, the Roman Catholic Parish Priest of Folkestone, the Librarian of the Vaughan Library at Harrow, are others to whom I am indebted for assistance in trying to trace the de Mauni family in England.

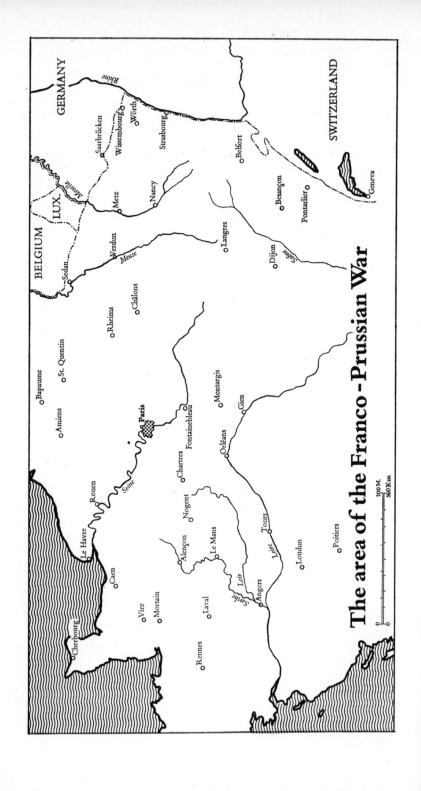

The area of the Franco-Prussian War

I

War Under the Empire— Saarbrücken to Sedan

'It is a common saying that nothing is sweeter than reflecting upon the storms of bygone days. If we cared only for the reminiscences of joy and glory, if happiness consisted in forgetting miseries which we have suffered and the disasters we have witnessed, then we should have to blot out from our memory the very smallest episode of the war in which France so nearly perished.

But human nature is not thus constituted; a kind of fascination rivets us to the sorrowful. There are only two things which can poison our recollections—shame and hate. Sufferings in which there is no consciousness of fault can never be unpleasant in retrospect.

Such was my thought when before the fire of a bivouac or in the shelter of a hut, I wrote from time to time the fugitive pages of this journal of the Battalion of Mortain, which my friends ask me now to put together. They know they cannot find in them any tale of victory, but we wish all of us to preserve the remembrance of the sufferings which we have endured, the unequal contests we have sustained, and the duty we have done to the best of our powers— memories full of sadness, but unstained by dishonour.

No one will blame a soldier of the Battalion of Mortain for having recorded what has passed under his eyes or was written from his knowledge, from the month of August 1870 to 26 March of this present year, with the reflections suggested to him by facts engraven for ever on his memory.

There are amongst many facts destined to oblivion, some episodes worthy of history. It cannot be waste of time to contribute, to the extent of one's knowledge, to an exact delineation of the course of our disaster.

I bring as my modest contribution, the simple record of what I have seen. The testimony of my companions in arms will answer for the accuracy of my narrative.'[1]

[1] From the Introduction to the *Memoirs of Roger de Mauni*.

The events which Roger de Mauni goes on to describe in his diary form part of the history of the twilight of the Franco-Prussian War. This war had been fated for a long time. It was certain that Prussia, in her rise to domination of the German States, must clash with France just as she had clashed with Austria. The Austrian campaign had taken place in 1866 and had culminated in the Prussian victory at Königgratz, or Sadowa as it is often known. With consummate statesmanship Bismarck had curbed the general desire for a triumphal march into Vienna and had insisted that there should be no demand for territorial reparations. In consequence, Austria had been beaten without being humiliatied and her allies had been left not unduly ill-disposed towards the victor. France had been hoodwinked into remaining inactive throughout the campaign, yet was sufficiently naïve to continue to hope that Austria and the South German States would side with her when it should come to her turn to play the victim. Bismarck, on the other hand, was looking to war with France as a means of binding the German States to Prussia, and meant to see that it came when he was ready.

The moment he was waiting for arrived in July 1870. The occasion was the offer of the Spanish throne to a Hohenzollern. King William was prepared to withdraw the Prussian candidature in the face of strong French opposition, but Bismarck had other ideas. By skilful manipulation of the wording of the notorious Ems telegram he contrived a *casus belli*; one, moreover, which laid the responsibility for further action on France. With scarcely a moment's hesitation, the French government accepted the bait and on 19 July declared war on Prussia.

There was little in the French military preparations to justify such eagerness. Although conscription was in force, it scarcely touched large sectors of the population, since exemption could be bought by the hire of substitutes. In 1867, Marshal Niel had recommended the formation of a national reserve to be known as the Garde Mobile, which was to consist of all men of military age who had not been selected for call-up to the regular forces and who, in consequence, had no obligation to serve in the regular reserve. The intention was that the Garde Mobile should be given two weeks' training a year. Niel was accused of attempting to turn France into one vast barracks; his critics, he retorted, were in danger of turning her into a vast cemetery. His training scheme was never implemented, but lists of names for the Garde Mobile were drawn up and in 1870 these men were called to the colours. Amongst them was Roger De Mauni.

'When I arrived at the Camp of Châlons, on 1 August, with the Mobile of the Seine, to which corps I belonged from having been drawn in the Paris conscription, the war was only just beginning, and misfortune had not yet made us serious. I remember the intense transports everywhere excited by the taking of Saarbrücken. The disasters of Wissembourg and Reichshoffen caused some emotion; but it was not till after Sedan that France really awakened from her dream.'

The dream in which France had been indulging was one in which her armies were back amongst the glories of the Napoleonic era. But Napoleon III was no Bonaparte, and in the intervening years France had somehow lost her military professionalism. Whilst during the latter half of July the Prussian forces mobilized quickly and efficiently in their territorial depots and moved forward by rail to their concentration areas in the Palatinate, the French army struggled against the confusion of a system which consigned men and equipment wildly in all directions. When, at the end of the month, the Emperor arrived at Metz to take command of the army in the field, he found his eight army corps widely dispersed, deficient in men and equipment, and without any idea of the enemy's whereabouts or intentions. Lacking any definite plan, after two days' hesitation he moved tentatively towards Saarbrücken. A few shells were fired at the railway station, but, in spite of what Roger de Mauni says, the town was never taken. The move served, however, to galvanise the Prussian armies. On 4 August 1870, the first elements crossed the frontier. Paradoxically the men were Bavarians, soldiers of one of the South German kingdoms which Napoleon III had hoped to lure away from the Prussian Alliance.

The Prussians were deployed in three armies. The supreme command was held by King William, but military control was exercised by the Chief of the General Staff, Count von Moltke. His plan of campaign was essentially simple; to advance with the three armies in line and to bring the opposing forces to battle wherever he found them. He intended to rely upon speed of concentration, superior discipline and better organisation to achieve a successful outcome. The first real contact took place at the little walled frontier town of Wissembourg, where an outlying division of Marshal

3

MacMahon's Corps was overwhelmed by the greatly superior forces of the Third Army under the command of the Prussian Crown Prince. Following up the fugitives, the Third Army next unexpectedly came upon the main body of MacMahon's Corps concentrated around Wörth and Reichshoffen, at the eastern approaches to one of the main passages through the Vosges mountains. The battle which developed piecemeal on 6 August resulted in the complete defeat of MacMahon's Corps, the remnants of which withdrew in disorder. They eventually reached, some ten days later, the great military camp at Châlons-sur-Marne, at the same time as Roger de Mauni was about to quit it.

Meanwhile on the other flank, the French had fared equally badly. By 8 August their forces were in full retreat toward the fortress town of Metz, pursued by the two other Prussian armies. Of these, the First followed a direct line while the Second swept round to the south. Only after crossing the Moselle did it turn northwards, with the result that it came between the French and their further line of withdrawal from Metz to the west. Marshal Bazaine, who by that time had been given command of all the forces in the area, intended to fight his way out westwards, but the presence of the fortress at his back induced a fatal indecisiveness. Although he could have broken out he elected instead to fight a defensive battle as if for protection of Metz. The struggle, which lasted three days, included such memorable actions as von Bredow's charge, the great cavalry engagements of Mars-la-Tour, Vionville and Rezonville, the murderous infantry battle across the ravine at Gravelotte and the slaughter of the Prussian Guard Corps at St Privat. At the end of it, both sides had lost heavily in men and material, but Bazaine was besieged in Metz.

The refugees from these disasters on either flank met at Châlons. From Reichshoffen came MacMahon with the remnants of his Corps and from Metz came the Emperor with the Prince Imperial and such few troops as had escaped the encirclement. Already in the camp were eighteen mutinous Garde Mobile battalions from the Seine and a new regular corps in process of formation under General Trochu. On the evidence of his brilliant earlier career, Trochu should by now at the age of fifty-six have been in command of an Army. But politically he was suspected of Orleanist leanings and temperamentally he was unambitious; he had also on occasions commented publicly on the weaknesses of the French army. Yet he was now destined to play a major part in the future of the war. News had come from Paris that a revolutionary situation was developing. It was essential to provide a firm military hand to support the Empress Eugénie, who was acting as Regent. As it was unthinkable that the Emperor himself should return to the capital in defeat, Trochu was selected to return as Governor charged with the defence of the city, and to take with him the Garde Mobile battalions. At the same time, it was decided that MacMahon should assume command of all the regular forces in the area in the name of the 'Army of Châlons' and that on 20 August he should march to Rheims to be in a position either to go to the relief of Metz or to fall back for the defence of Paris, as the situation demanded. With him went the Emperor, no longer in command but as a passenger for whom there was nowhere else to go.

MacMahon was in a terrible dilemma. Reason told him that he should save his force and fall back to defend Paris, but all the advice from the capital was that revolution would break out if he appeared to be abandoning Bazaine. He was misled too about Bazaine's real situation by unfounded reports that a break-out was still possible. His consequent hesitations and slowness gave time for the Prussian forces to regroup and to resume their westward movement. Leaving adequate forces to besiege Metz, a new army, known as the Army of the Meuse, had been formed. This, together with the Third Prussian Army (the victors of Reichshoffen), continued the advance. With these forces von Moltke planned to annihilate MacMahon wherever he should find him.

By 30 August, MacMahon had decided that there was no longer any hope of effecting a junction with Bazaine and that he must withdraw towards Paris. After a major engagement at Beaumont and several days' hard fighting along the Meuse, however, he had first to concentrate and rest his troops, even though the enemy were at his heels. Just to the north lay the town of Sedan. He had no choice but to enter it, trusting that he could hold the high ground immediately around it for sufficiently long to keep a route open to the west. But even as the French troops moved in the Prussian forces began to encircle the area.

By the evening of the next day the battle was over. MacMahon was wounded. The Emperor delivered his sword to the King of Prussia, while von Moltke and Bismarck drafted the terms of surrender. On 2 September 1870, Napoleon III passed into captivity and with him nearly all that remained of the French regular forces, less those besieged in Metz or in the other fortress towns still holding out. A few escaped from Sedan, like General Ducrot who was to fight on in Paris, and the Prince Imperial who eventually joined the Empress in exile in England.

The news of the defeat put the capital in turmoil. As the Empire slipped into oblivion, republicans of all hues and denominations closed in on the Hôtel de Ville and the Assemblée Nationale. On 4 September the Republic was declared. In the general scramble for position and the excitement of a bloodless revolution, the enemy was forgotten, or, if he was remembered, it was with the assumption that now the Emperor had gone the war was over. Now indeed was the time for an act of magnanimity on the part of Bismarck such as had ended the Austrian war. Prussia had achieved her object; the French regular forces were utterly defeated, the Empire was destroyed and there was no longer any doubt as to which was the most powerful nation in Europe. But the Prussian military leaders were greedy for territorial concessions to guarantee the security of the frontier for ever. If the Republican government would not surrender them now, the Prussians were able and prepared to advance further into France. Confident that neither Britain nor any other European power would intervene, they calculated that the fall of Paris would shortly bring to an end all resistance. At the same time, on the other side, the new leaders saw clearly that the surrender of any part of the homeland would mean the end of the Republic. Its strength lay in becoming the symbol and means of resistance to the invader. Jules Favre truly reflected the feeling of the people when he promised to surrender neither a stone of her fortresses nor a single inch of French territory. Closely linked with these sentiments was the fate of Roger de Mauni and of thousands like him.

Eight Months on Duty

Mourmelon (from a seventh-class hotel)

Wednesday morning, 3 August 1870

My dear Mother,

The morning after you left me, I went to the roll-call, where we were kept for an hour and a half. At four o'clock we assembled at the Invalides, with our knapsacks, cloaks, bread, mess-bowls, and tin cans at our backs—a burden weighing more than forty pounds. On our way to the station the populace were very demonstrative. The *gamins* came and offered to carry our knapsacks—a favour which many of us accepted. Our march was very fatiguing, for we were stifling under our woollen shirts and thick cloth tunics, to say nothing of our knapsacks. The *gamins* accompanied us, breaking our ranks, and joining in the songs of the Mobiles, shouting the *Marseillaise* and *Mourir pour la Patrie* during a great part of the distance. I kept aloof from all these manifestations, and held no communication with the populace, for it all jarred upon me greatly. I had been separated from Auger de Madron, and marched alone on my side of the road in the midst of the riff-raff who were following us. Monsieur de Vernou-Bonneuil was leading the way, mounted on a fine charger. Some of the *gamins* began to cry 'Vive Rochefort!'[1] but we sternly imposed silence upon them. One very great cry was 'A Cayenne Ollivier!'[2] It was a curious scene; but my heart was oppressed by hearing all these follies and horrors uttered by such coarse, discordant voices.

At Aubervilliers we had some refreshments, and then got into an immense train of third-class carriages, very hard, but with plenty of room. We were ten hours on the road, crawling along like a luggage train. We could not sleep; we laughed and shouted instead. My companions were most kind and pleasant.

A branch line runs from Châlons to the village of Mourmelon. We arrived there at four a.m., very much fatigued; but we had to take up our knapsacks, and march six kilometres in full sunshine after our sleepless night.

On reaching the camp, Monsieur de Rivoire told us that there was a superfluous number of men in the first company, and that those who wished to enter the second had only to say so. The instant the roll-call was over, I flew in search of F. de Rougé. I found him establishing himself with F. de Bastard, MM. Robert and Gontran de Montesquiou, and some other agreeable companions in a tent holding ten or twelve. We had a great deal of trouble before we could get some old straw mattresses to lay on the ground, and at last sink down upon them to rest.

[1] Henri de Rochefort, an extreme Republican, who was to play a leading role in the Commune.

[2] Emile Ollivier, President of the Council, shortly to fall from power as a result of the first French defeats.

The camp at Châlons is an immense chalky plain, dotted with clumps of trees, and bounded in the distance by a chain of high hills. The space occupied by the troops would give, I should think, a diameter of at least two leagues.[1]

We go by the name of 'the Battalion of Varnished Boots'. We are a united band, my friends and I, and we help one another in making our life here as pleasant as we can.

I send you a sketch of our tents. Those of the officers are like the others, except that they are occupied only by two, and contain iron bedsteads, whilst we are ten in each tent, and sleep in a circle, with our feet turned towards the centre, which is lower than the surrounding part. In the middle is the pole supporting the tent, and to which are fastened the twine and pegs and shelves which hold our possessions. A small trench is dug round it, to carry off the rain-water. It did us great service last night, when we had a violent thunderstorm. Without some precautions we should have been deluged.

We are gradually getting rested, and settling down into our new way of living. It seems to me a century since we came here, so much have we passed through.

Adieu, dear mother. I embrace you very affectionately, and am always yours respectfully and devotedly. My companions are making such a noise, that I scarcely know what I am writing.

Roger

Camp at Châlons, Friday morning, 5 August 1870

My dear Mother,

I received your delightful letter of six pages yesterday, and Louise's also. You may imagine what happiness it gave me to read your loving words. I too am often with you in thought, and feel our separation deeply. We are beginning to get used to all the inconveniences of our position. Many of my comrades were very much fatigued, but all are now recovering.

I look forward with joy to the possibility of your coming to see us; but so long as we are not quartered in a town it cannot be thought of. Mourmelon is a detestable place, wretched and dirty, where you would soon be ill, and where you could not think of bringing Louise or Constance. I have not seen one lady yet who deserves the name.

[1] A league is four kilometres or two and a half miles.

No place is habitable in which a number of ill-conditioned men are collected together, so much is one's moral and physical sense revolted by everything one sees and hears; it strikes death into the soul. You never hear the name of God but amidst blasphemies, nor of woman but with some odious epithet attached to it.

The night before last we had an illumination for the taking of Saarbrücken. You know more of our political and military events than I do, for it is very seldom we get any papers, and very few of us look at them. Bismarck, represented by a comical-looking figure stuffed with squibs and crackers, was burnt in effigy. The sight of the illuminated camp from the top of the church tower at Mourmelon, which is very high, was beautiful.

As to Châlons, it is a long way off, and no one ever goes there.

We are forty thousand men in the camp, of whom a great number consist of troops of the line, who are every day expecting to be ordered off to the Rhine.

I have not forgotten my village friends, but you have absorbed all my thoughts since we parted.

It is a great happiness to us to be so many together from the same district; it makes a great difference in our position. We keep up an unbroken friendship. The rule all for one is taken here in its best sense, and each individual difficulty is turned or vanquished by a collective effort.

Excuse my careless writing, dear mother, for I am very sleepy. I had begun a letter to my father, but the rain destroyed it, so that I must put off sending it till tomorrow.

Châlons-sur-Marne, 20 August 1870

The news of the first defeat of our armies surprised us at Rheims, in the midst of a gay party of pleasure. We had gone, a number of us together, to see the town which is eight leagues from from the camp, and to breakfast at the Lion d'Or, in the Place de la Cathédrale. The first moments of consternation over, we soon recovered our national gaiety; and from that time till our return to Paris we were every day deluded with reports of victories, and it was only at rare intervals that our lightheartedness was interrupted by some glimpses of the truth. . . . Our chief anxiety was to find a place at the table-d'hôte, and at the next café-concert.

9

I do not suppose that in any place in which a large number of men have been collected together for an important object, so complete a contrast between the grave and the gay, the ludicrous and the awful has ever been presented as at the camp of Châlons during the first three weeks of August 1870.

At 4 a.m., drums beating and bugles sounding the reveille announced the end of a bitterly cold night. This immense plain, which extends over more than twenty-five leagues between Rheims and Troyes, is, even in the height of summer, swept by the most piercing wind. There is no shelter from the sun by day, nor from icy blasts when night sets in. It is like the climate of the seaside with the same abrupt variations.

Till six, we dressed and made our coffee. Then the summons to muster round the colours called all the battalions to the main front line. When all the Gardes Mobiles of the Seine were assembled, we were about fifteen thousand men; our line of battle was more than a quarter of a league in length.

After muster came drill. For four hours we were marched either in a column of sections or in file, up and down those sterile plains, which are peopled only by a few miserable-looking flocks and herds, and scantily planted with stunted fir-trees. We had soon attained some proficiency in the art of marching, and also in the execution of the first simple manoeuvres, and we had learnt also how to handle a *fusil à tabatière*.[1] Parisians are not slow in learning. As to discipline, we prided ourselves on ignoring the word altogether. We gave it clearly to be understood that we were not soldiers, but the Mobile National Guard. We expected to be treated with respect, and to be commanded with politeness. Consequently the most complete antagonism existed between the officers in command and the citizens they were endeavouring to convert into soldiers. Entire liberty of speech and unlimited discussion of orders appeared to the Garde Mobile of the Seine the most sacred of rights. On the other hand, there were some officers who seemed to regard it as their chief duty to exercise the men in humility and patience (those virtues so eminently un-Parisian), and to accustom them to receive the harshest reprimands in silence. Some well-bred young men there were among the captains and lieutenants, who treated their subordinates with exquisite urbanity, abstaining from the infliction of all punishments, and exhibiting on every occasion that modesty which is the characteristic of intelligent inexperience. These officers

[1] Flint lock musket.

were popular, but scarcely escaped the reproach of incapacity which is so often the reward of all absence of pretension.

On one of the first days in August, Marshal Canrobert[1] came to review the battalions which had already arrived. There had been some disturbances, and he uttered a few severe words. Instantly his voice was drowned by tumultuous cries and shouts; he saw that he had got out of his element and hastily withdrew. . . .

The Garde Mobile of the Seine was composed of very diverse elements. The battalions levied in certain *faubourgs* were little better than mere bands of brigands, with just a handful of respectable characters. But those of the central districts—the seventh, for instance—contained a larger proportion of young men who were well educated, and imbued with a sense of honour and duty, than could be found in most other regiments. It cannot be said that any of them, whichever class they belonged to, were wanting in physical courage; but the greater number of them showed a profound horror of anything approaching to enthusiasm, devotion, or greatness of soul. Our chief desire was, not to be heroes, but to pass for sagacious and clever politicians. Zeal was universally condemned, and reason alone was in the ascendant. Logic was appealed to in discussions of all sorts of subjects; the word was on everyone's lips, and was commonly employed by minds, however illogically constituted, in deciding the questions of the day. There was in every heart, together with a certain sense of personal dignity, a strong element of egotism, an insane dread of being tricked or made capital of, and that fantastic hatred of the existing Government for which the Parisian always professes to have the best of reasons.

The morning manoeuvres being over, we returned to the camp, filling the air with songs more or less jubilant, amongst which the *Marseillaise* held a conspicuous place. Then all the companies repaired to their respective kitchens, to receive their rations of soup—each man's portion being poured into his own porringer. At noon the bugles again sounded, and the sergeant-majors made the roll-call;

[1] One of the more colourful French commanders. Like MacMahon, he had fought in the Crimea and was a legend with the Armée d'Afrique, both for his personal bravery and for his shoulder-length hair, which he refused to cut short on the grounds that 'these locks will go down to history'. Although sufficiently senior to be granted command of an Army, he knew his limitations and was content with that of a corps. He commanded 6 Corps which formed at Châlons and joined Bazaine for the battle of Metz. This Corps held the position at St Privat, where terrible losses were inflicted on the Prussian Guard Corps as they advanced in columns across the open fields.

after which there was the corporal's drill and other military duties; and so the hours dragged their weary length along till four.

In less than a week this army, divided into a number of marching regiments,[1] had become completely organised. The list of commissioned officers having been in great measure made out some time before, the battalions were from the first day provided with adjutants, majors, and quartermasters, most of them old soldiers tolerably well acquainted with their duties. Clothing and equipments had been furnished at the outset; and as the Paris Mobiles considered themselves delivered up to the enemy, bound hand and foot, because they were armed with only Sneider guns, the authorities hastened to furnish them with *chassepots*[2] by the end of August. I believe no battalion that has since been levied in the provinces was so well supplied from the first with all that was requisite.

At the hour at which I am now writing the ashes of the German bivouac fires are no doubt strewn over the place where stood that city of tents, so populous, so animated. Nothing could be more curious than the aspect of that whole region, where men had gathered together, round the immense apparatus for their mutual destruction, the paraphernalia of every kind of pleasure. As the day drew on the two long streets forming the village of Grand-Mourmelon were filled with a vociferous multitude, consisting of Mobiles, soldiers of the line, women, chaplains, doctors, and, after the first battles, all the stragglers and disabled from MacMahon's army[3]—dismounted horsemen, gunners who had lost their pieces, famished and unintelligible Turcos,[4] and that herd of indefinable characters, for whom the word *goujat* was invented by our forefathers. All these people came to eat, to drink, to while away their time, and to make purchases. Every house in Mourmelon was turned into a shop, and also into a place of amusement, where shouting, singing, and quarrelling went on from three o'clock

---

[1] Misleading translation of Régiments de Marche. The title denotes non-regular regiments. A regiment consisted normally of three battalions each of six companies, each of about 130 men.

[2] The *chassepot* was far and away the best rifle of its period and much superior to the German 'needle-gun'. Breech-loading, it was sighted to 1,300 yards and accurate against individual targets up to 400 yards. Its rate of fire was seven to eight rounds a minute and it could be fitted with the long bayonet.

[3] The remnants of the French Corps which had been defeated at Reichshoffen and Wörth on 6 August.

[4] Generic name for Algerian or Moroccan infantry.

in the afternoon till nightfall. And in the midst of these bazaars and haunts of dissipation rose the church, its vaulted roof re-echoing with the chants of the Benediction service, whilst up to its very gates came the din of all this bacchanalian clamour. At 9 p.m. all was again silent and deserted; but on returning to the camp the noise and tumult began worse than ever, and was often kept up till far on into the night. The heaps of wood and straw blazing all along the line—the mannequins filled with crackers, exploding in every direction in long jets of fire—the blue flames of the great bowls of punch, flaring here and there in front of the tents, illuminated the pathways with a thousand different lights. Mingled with the sounds of revelry might be heard the sinister yells of Belleville[1] ruffians, who were prowling about the camp in search of riot and disturbance. Sometimes there was bloodshed, and the offenders fled into the darkness.

All this time, if we were to believe the newspapers and newsmongers, our armies had been marching from one success to another. On 15 August, a victory at Longueville[2] was universally reported, and part of the camp was illuminated. This life lasted till 18 August. For some days it had been rumoured that the Mobiles of the Seine were to be sent to guard the fortified towns on the east. The indignation of the soldier-citizens at the idea of having to defend their country was a spectacle as ridiculous as it was odious. On the 17th the circle was formed, and it was officially announced to us that we were to return to Paris. Those who had cherished a moment's hope that they were to be sent to the front were deeply depressed and mortified at this retreat. Our brave Major Vernon-Bonneuil read the order in a voice choked with emotion. His words were received with an uproarious shout of joy, and instantly thousands of excited voices made the camp ring with shouts ,'To Paris!'

The next day we took the road to Rheims. Before starting we had to give up our knapsacks, which were required for the equipment of Marshal MacMahon's corps.[3] We wrapped up our possessions in our

[1] Belleville was an area of workers' slums in the north-eastern part of Paris.

[2] This must be the village of Longueville which lies two miles west of Metz on the road to Gravelotte. French Imperial Headquarters was established there on 15 August during the withdrawal across the Moselle. On that morning the Prussian artillery began to shell the village, which was choked with baggage wagons. The Emperor and the Prince Imperial made their way on foot to Gravelotte. There was no victory.

[3] The troops, who as part of the Army of Châlons, were to accompany MacMahon to Sedan.

rugs, and the heavy bales were placed in carts. From the camp to the station at Rheims the distance is from eight to nine leagues. The first four were easily accomplished; there was nothing but cries of joy, noisy jests, and ribald songs, which our heroes sang unblushingly with the *Marseillaise* and the *Rhin Allemand*. But as the evening came on the effects of fatigue began to appear; the sounds of gaiety became less and less obstreperous; hunger, thirst, and dust are infallible sedatives for the marching man. The long column which, when it first started in two files along the sides of the road, looked like a joyous masquerading party, fell at last into a confused throng—uttering groans, complaints, and imprecations. The annoyance and disgust we had felt at first gave way to compassion. When we got to the station we piled arms, whilst waiting for the train. We sat down on the ground round the great station-yard. Some had still strength left to go in search of a drop of water and a morsel of bread. Many remained for two hours without stirring, in the place where they had sunk down in the mire. At length the order for entering the train was given. Everyone found energy enough to run and secure a place before all was full. In a few seconds the confusion was at its height. No order could be heard, and the crowd, left to itself, was struggling and fighting round the carriages. Armed ruffians, yelling with rage, were kicking against the doors, and threatening with their bayonets everyone who refused to make way for them. The dread of being left behind was the one prevailing thought. The journey lasted the whole night and part of the next day; our long train, incessantly stopping, made the slowest progress. . . .

On our arrival in Paris a proclamation was read to us on parade from General Trochu.[1] 'You have been brought back to Paris,' he said, 'as it is your right to be.' We did not then know that Paris was to sustain a long siege, and that the plains of Châlons were to be deliberately given up to the Prussians; and this 'right', so unheard of, granted to the inhabitants of a town, by which they were excused from contributing to the defence of the provinces, excited great indignation amongst us.[2]

My fellow Mobiles re-entered Paris with transports of joy. There

[1] Trochu had returned from Châlons on 18 August as Governor charged with the defence of the capital.

[2] There was, in fact, no reason why the Garde Mobile should not be called upon to serve anywhere, once they had mustered and equipped. They were not departmental troops, such as the Garde Nationale Sédentaire.

are those for whom the boulevards are France. A cabinet-maker from my quarter, when the Barrière du Trône came in sight, very nearly burst into tears. In spite of my affection for Paris, I had taken all the steps necessary to be appointed officer in a department where the list of Gardes Mobiles was not yet filled up. On arriving at the camp at St Maur I heard that I was made a lieutenant.

Mortain, Thursday, 25 August 1870

I arrived the night before last in this little town, with its dark and narrow streets built amongst rocks and precipices in the midst of a wild country, three leagues from the frontier of Brittany. Everything now around me is as different as it can be from what I left two days ago.

At half past six in the morning the drums pass by, with a tremendous noise, under the windows of the Hôtel de la Poste. There is just time to dress in haste, and get to the Place de la Sous-Préfecture, where the battalion is assembling. Crowds of young men in blouses and jackets, caps and hats, are thronging the streets, going where their duty calls them. Most of them have the amused and interested look of men who are trying a trade for the first time in their lives; very few have the dull, wearied expression of countenance I have observed so often.

I have not yet had a sight of the major. He is ill, and confined to his room. I have been introduced to those officers who were on the Place. The commissions are all filled up, but some of those who have been appointed have not yet arrived. We have only five or six here in uniform.[1]

When the sergeant-majors had called the roll, and given each man his pay of twenty sous, the eight companies started, all in different directions, for their drill. The third, to which I belong, ascended a steep hill in good order, and drew up on a road. Fields in which we can manoeuvre are scarce in this hilly country.

The battalion is very large, each division numbering about 200 men. Those with me are mostly agriculturists, founders, or travelling tinkers. They are in general tall, well-built men—their country faces beaming with health and vigour. When we get our arms, clothing,

---

[1] The battalion on 31 August numbered 1,442 men. The uniform of the Garde Mobiles was képi, blue frock coat, and grey trousers.

képis, 'books', knapsacks, and tents, we shall be a goodly battalion; but as yet we are unprovided with a single thing.

These Normans are certainly not so quick as the Parisians at comprehending 'right turn' and 'right-about turn'; but they show a better will, and are by nature more inclined to arms. I doubt if, a month hence, they would have anything to learn from the Mobiles of the Seine. It would be curious to compare them, if, according to the prevailing rumour, we should be sent to Paris. In the meantime the relief is inexpressible of being no longer on a scorching plain, having to listen to a constant nonsensical chatter about 'logic' and 'republic', kept up by those who are incapable of reasoning, and with whom justice is the last of their aspirations.

The mornings are delightful on this green hillside—looking out over the luxuriant plain, which stretches far away into the distance—and in the midst of all these bright young warriors, so gay, so impetuous, so heedless, and so swift to run a race too, when they get leave from their captain to go and drink a *moque* of cider at the neighbouring inn. As yet they have been all kindness and amiability. Their goodwill seems to ascribe to me, in virtue of my new uniform, much greater merits than I can at all lay claim to. As for my captain, I do not know whether he likes me, but I am sure that I like him. It is no wonder if, in explaining the theory of war, he should at times use the gestures of a barrister, since he is imperial attorney in Mortain. He is a slight man, of middle height and florid complexion, with black hair, and beard; he looks very intelligent, kind, and unaffected. He takes great pains with us. He is a volunteer, and, from what I see, had no need to become a soldier to hold a distinguished place in any public office.

The evening here is very much the same as the morning. We drill from three to five, after which every one is set at liberty. The men are billeted on the inhabitants in and about the town.

Saturday, 27 August

No news. The despatches are obscure. The fate of the battalion of Mortain seems very uncertain. Will the Government employ us at last, or are we in danger of being left disregarded in this little Norman Switzerland, eight leagues from the railway, and twenty from any large town? One thing which has certainly been forgotten is, that we are absolutely destitute of everything in the shape of accoutrements or outfit. But still we do our best, and we are becoming as military as men can be without muskets or pompons. The day is passed in manoeuvring exercises, and in the corporals' and sergeants' schools. The officers are soon to have their own course of instruction. A police-station has been established, and a mess at the hotel was organised yesterday by my captain.

Sunday, 28 August

I spent the day in getting acquainted with this country, where I had never been before. This Norman 'bush',[1] far removed as it is from every railway line, is one of the happiest regions in the world. Everything here is old and peaceful; the farmhouses, strongly built of granite or schist, are surrounded with venerable old trees. I saw in a remote corner, behind the hedges and orchards, the roof where M. de Frotte, the chief of the Norman Chouans, was for a long time sheltered from the pursuit of the Blues.[2] Highroads are scarce; the thoroughfares most in use are the hollow roads of our ancestors. They lie between huge banks, eight or ten feet high and crowned with bramble hedges, often interspersed with big trees. The 'heritages' are divided by similar enclosures, which have doubtless been established ages ago. The plain, seen from a distance, looks like one thick mass of brushwood, where a nation determined to fight for its liberty would easily make an impregnable position for itself. Nowhere is shooting over fields a harder or more fatiguing sport. It is, however, eagerly pursued by the young men around, and the partridge season is impatiently waited for. There is rarely any coursing. The deer are few, and the roebucks of the forest mostly see their lives ended by a bullet. The wolves have not disappeared from these wild regions;[3] they prowl at times at no great distance from human dwellings. There is no lack of boars and foxes.

The towns here are very small, and yet they are not dull to live in; the inhabitants seem to get on very well by themselves, and to find enjoyment at home. Mortain has not more than 3,000 inhabitants. The old gentry, and the almost equally old bourgeoisie, live there side

---

[1] *Le bocage*, a term which was to become terribly familiar again in 1944.

[2] Soldiers of the Republic.

[3] Surprising but quite true at that period.

by side, and contrive to bear very well with each other. By the seaside, Granville and Avranches are the centres of commerce and amusement, where, in summer, those fortunate enough to have leisure go for the sake of sea-bathing and meeting their friends. English visitors from Jersey often disembark on this hospitable shore, where they find cheerful welcome, fine walks, and cheap living. People come to Avranches from great distances to enjoy the magnificent view in the Episcopal Garden. As far as the eye can reach the bay of Mont St Michel displays its flat beach, over which the tide rushes twice a day with fearful rapidity. Mont St Michel and the romantic islet of Tombelaine command the alternately sandy and liquid plain, surrounded as with a green and shadowy belt by the Norman and Breton hills.

The people hold to their religious traditions. The clergy are zealous and earnest, and have reason to be satisfied with the piety of their people. A few days ago, the Curé of Mortain having announced that there would be benediction with the blessed sacrament in the evening, our fellows went there in hundreds. The walls of the old church re-echoed with their vigorous voices, chanting the hymns of their villages. This devotion, though sometimes allied to rather independent morals, gives nevertheless an exquisite impression to those coming out of the materialist and infidel mob among which we have spent three weeks. This race has still heart and honour and energy, and I am sure it is a match for the flower of Teutonia. Give us only time to prepare for the fight.

The society of the small towns mixes with that of the châteaux, where much intimacy, simplicity, and liveliness are to be found. One must not look here for the hideous picture of provincial hatreds and jealousies described by Balzac. If the order of departure we are expecting does not call us away for ever, we shall return to visit these lovely regions and get acquainted with their inhabitants.

Wednesday, 31 August

Some carts arrived this morning, laden with old percussion guns. There is, as might have been expected, general disappointment. For my part, I scarcely expected anything better. Yet it is inconceivable how the Ministry of War should not take into account the hurtful effects sure to be produced by an unequal distribution of arms among the troops. It seems as if they would rather sacrifice the men's lives than incur the expense of a few extra halfpence. The moral inferiority which will be the consequence, when we are brought face to face with the enemy, will be even more disastrous than the undeniable material disadvantage involved. The major announced to us today that we were henceforth to belong to the 30th 'Régiment de Marche', which means that we shall soon probably be called to active service. How, then, will it be possible to persuade our Mobiles that they are to fight as boldly as the soldiers of the line by their side, when the latter are provided with guns which have a range twice as long as their own, and far more accurate, and which can be loaded four times as expeditiously? Hopes are held out to us that this is only a provisional arrangement. It is much to be desired, for the instruction of the battalion, that we may soon have our regular accoutrements.

Friday, 2 September

If our equipment goes on at this rate, we shall not be ready till the war is over. Seven hundred very inferior képis arrived this morning; these are not enough for half the men. They were given out under a pouring rain, which soon reduced the cardboard they are made of into a soft pulp. Marshal Le Boeuf was decidedly a little mistaken when he declared that France was 'ready'.[1]

The news of the war is confused and contradictory. Here, where things are not quite so lightly taken as they are at Paris, people are beginning to feel anxious, and I think not without some cause.

Monday, 5 September

Two days of great anxiety and grief. Yesterday morning, just as we were all considering how we could make the most of our Sunday holiday, the town-crier suddenly appeared in the market-place, proclaiming the defeat of MacMahon's army and the capture of

---

[1] Le Boeuf, when war was declared, had assured the nation that the French Army was 'ready to the last gaiter-button'. He was the same Le Boeuf who some ten years before had been responsible for simplifying the French artillery timed fuse, so that in 1870 the French shells could be set to explode at only one of two ranges, while the Prussian percussion shells burst on impact at all ranges.

the Emperor with forty thousand men! At night the news came to the telegraph office that the Republic was proclaimed in Paris, with Rochefort as a member of the new Government. I went to bed, thinking that my country was indeed hastening with rapid strides towards her ruin, since, to the disasters of foreign invasion, the curses of internal strife were now so soon likely to be added. The French people will always be the same; they destroy the Government of their own creation when it is no time for establishing another, hoping by this act of madness to put an end to all their misfortunes, and to justify all their errors.

I observe that, however innocent the thing may be which it represents, yet there is something exceedingly dangerous in the word 'Republic'. Both in Paris and in the provinces it is a signal for complete licence: like schoolboys suddenly let loose, we no sooner hear it than we begin to make all the uproar that we can. This is what we have seen today, in one of the most peaceful and secluded parts of France. This morning our lads, when they went to drill, began by striking up the *Marseillaise*, the Bretons from Saint-Hilaire shouting more furiously than the rest. One of them went in search of a plaster head, which had fallen from a decapitated bust of the Emperor, and stuck it on the point of his bayonet. It was impossible to persuade them that it was not a very heroic action. Some of the officers inquired whether the offenders should be arrested; but the major considered it more prudent not to add to the present excitement by too sudden a display of severity. He came down to the Place on foot, looking pale and rigid; he measured the battalion with one stern glance, and then ordered the men off to drill. They obeyed on the instant. At the afternoon muster there was a slight repetition of the disturbance; but the storm gradually lulled of its own accord, and this evening the town is tolerably quiet again. I do not know what are the major's intentions, but I believe he has acted wisely in doing nothing at all. . . .

II

The Start of the People's War

In spite of Roger de Mauni's forebodings, there was to be practically no civil dissension. The fall of the Empire was so sudden and so complete that its Ministers just sank out of sight and any remaining supporters of the regime were left without a rallying point. Quickly, too, the Republican government gained patriotic support by becoming identified directly with the protection of the homeland and with the continued resistance to the invader. It is true that an attempt at peace was made, but after meeting with Bismarck Jules Favre was convinced that there was no alternative but to continue the war, and it was Gambetta who coined the phrase *la guerre à outrance*.

Both sides were certain that Paris was the key to further resistance. Leaving behind enough troops to escort the prisoners from Sedan, von Moltke pressed on towards the capital. His plan was to surround the city and cut off supplies; he never contemplated a direct attack, since the General Staff's estimate of the likely period of resistance under siege varied from eight days to a maximum of a few weeks. By 20 September the city was completely encircled.

The French, on the other hand, had no doubts of the ability of the capital to hold out as long as there was food. They calculated the supplies within the city as sufficient for twelve weeks. This was an underestimate, which was to a degree to distort their future strategy, but whatever the amount the siege would have to be broken sooner or later if the city was not to be starved into surrender. Responsibility for the defence of the city rested with Trochu, appointed Governor of Paris and recently elected President of the Republic. The command of such forces as could be used for a break-out was entrusted to General Ducrot, who to the joy of Trochu had appeared in Paris in mid-September having escaped while *en route* to the east as a prisoner after Sedan. Whilst the Government should properly have been in a place where it could communicate with the outside world, reasons of morale demanded that it should remain in the capital. A governmental delegation

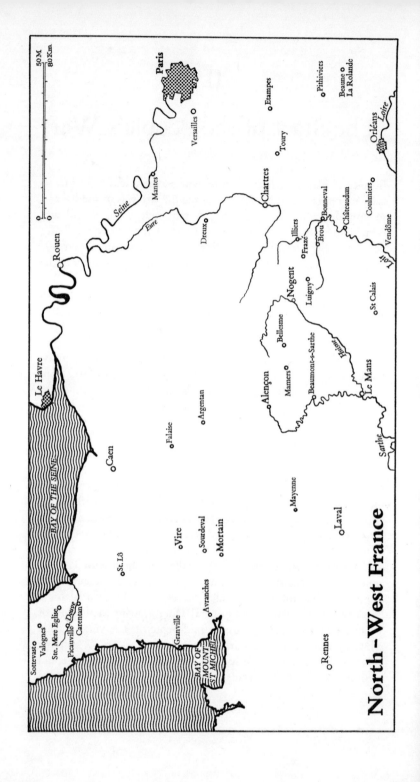

North–West France

50 M
80 Km

Paris

Versailles

Étampes

Pithiviers

Beaune
La Rolande

Orléans

Toury

Loire

Mantes

Chartres

Dreux

Illiers

Frazé

Brou

Bonneval

Châteaudun

Coulmiers

Vendôme

Seine

Eure

Nogent

Luigny

St Calais

Loir

Rouen

Le Havre

Bellesme

Beaumont-s-Sarthe

Mamers

Le Mans

Huisne

Alençon

Argentan

Sarthe

Falaise

Caen

BAY OF THE SEINE

Mayenne

Vire

Sourdeval

Mortain

Laval

St. Lô

Sottevast

Valognes

Ste. Mère Eglise

Picauville

Carentan

Douve

Granville

Avranches

BAY OF
MOUNT
ST. MICHEL

Rennes

was in consequence despatched to Tours with the task of organising the defence of the provinces and of raising forces for the relief of Paris from outside.

There was no shortage of troops of various kinds within the city, including the 15,000 unruly but partially trained Gardes Mobiles who had been at Châlons with Roger de Mauni. But outside Paris there was no regular front-line unit in France, except those besieged in the various fortresses, until three regiments of infantry were brought back from Algiers. These formed the nucleus of a new corps, 15 Corps, which was being formed in the Loire district and which by the end of September had reached a strength of about 60,000 men. In the north-west General Fierrec was assembling battalions of the Garde Mobile into a force around Rouen and in the south-east an army was being gathered at Besançon. There were plenty of men, but everything else was lacking. To start with it is said that there were only six field guns in the whole of France ready for service. There were no maps. There was no organisation in the military department at Tours, not even an Intelligence bureau. What was worse, by the beginning of October political dissension and lack of confidence had developed between the Central Government and the Delegation. Direct control was exceedingly difficult as all the normal means of communication between Paris and the outside world had become impossible. In spite of the ingenious use of semaphore, balloons, carrier pigeons and other methods, there were to be times when the capital was completely cut off for long periods. In view of these difficulties, it was felt that a full member of the Government must go to Tours. The choice fell on Gambetta. On 9 October the Minister of the Interior, as he had then become, reached the provincial capital on the Loire after a hazardous journey by balloon. His dynamic personality and restless energy were to change the whole aspect of the war in the provinces.

The Germans, being committed to the siege of Metz and now having undertaken the siege of Paris, had very few troops left free to carry out mobile operations. In consequence, they had so far been able to do little to interfere with the French preparations and assembly of fresh forces. In addition, they had had to abandon their earlier fiction that their quarrel was only with the armies of the Emperor. They were now at war with the French people; as a result their cavalry patrols were no longer able to roam freely about the countryside and intelligence was much harder to get. Yet Gambetta realised that this period of relative impunity was unlikely to last. The fall of Strasbourg on 28 September, which freed the besieging troops for other tasks, gave a hint of what was to come. By 10 October, too, the first real brush had taken place between the newly formed 15 Corps and regular Bavarian troops north of Orleans. Although the French Corps had fallen back out of contact, the number of new forces on the Loire must soon be revealed.

The first thing that Gambetta did on arrival at Tours was to take upon himself the appointment of Minister for War in addition to his other duties as Minister of the Interior, and to appoint, as his most able and efficient delegate, a civil engineer named Charles de Freycinet. Next, he replaced the commander of 15 Corps by General d'Aurelle de Paladines, a regular soldier of some sixty-six years of age. This was to prove a less happy choice. Third, he worked out and published instructions for hampering enemy movement. Any Department within 100 kilometres of the invader was to be declared to be on war footing. Information about the march of the enemy would be sent direct to the military chiefs and Prefects within a radius of at least 100 kilometres in the direction of march. The military chiefs would then invoke a military committee, which would decide when and where the enemy should be engaged. The forces would be drawn from the regular or auxiliary troops of the Department not required for the operations of the Army Corps in the field, and the military chiefs would be held responsible for resistance to the enemy.

Finally, he considered what strategy should be pursued by the new regular forces. In addition to 15 Corps these now consisted of a new formation, 16 Corps, forming around Blois and Marchénoir, in the Loire valley, and several effective and sizeable independent units of franc-tireurs. All these together formed the Army of the Loire. It was decided that this Army, under the general command of d'Aurelle de Paladines, should advance directly on Paris via Orleans, with a view to linking up with an attack from within which Ducrot signalled he would be ready to make by 6 November. Speed was essential, as there were already ugly rumours spreading from the direction of Metz that Bazaine was treating with the enemy, and that his surrender was a possibility.

To oppose this advance there was known to be the Bavarian

First Corps under the command of General von der Tann in Orleans. It was thought that there were also sizeable German forces around Chartres. This was in fact not so, but to cover this flank there was General Fierrec's Army of the West. This was never in fact a formal grouping of forces such as the Army of the Loire, but a collection of franc-tireurs, Gardes Mobiles, Gardes Nationales and armed inhabitants with a small infusion of regular battalions, some marines, some mountain guns and one engineer battalion. Yet their commander made such skilful use of the close hilly country in which he operated that they gave the impression of being a much larger and more composite formation than in fact they were. It was to this army that for the moment belonged the 30th Régiment de Marche and the Battalion of Mortain. Roger de Mauni describes the preparation of the battalion and its first moves towards action.

Mortain, Tuesday, 6 September

Order is re-established. These Mobiles are giddy fellows, but there is no real harm in them; besides, the pouring rain keeps them safe indoors.

Wednesday, 7 September

It would be annoying if riots were to become a chronic evil amongst us; but we must not complain, for what is here a great event was our daily bread at Châlons. Today the organisation of war companies and the formation of the depot have been made the occasion of a regular tumult. It cannot be denied that the civil administration has been doing its best to cause general irritation by omitting (either from forgetfulness or favouritism) to call out a great many of the youths who were most fit for service. Such acts of injustice are very exasperating to those who are the sufferers, and it is only natural it should be so. Some of them undertook to send a petition on the subject to the chief authorities. At our age we are not given to gentle ways, and the signing of that paper—a process in itself of an exceedingly pacific nature—became the cause of a great uproar. A lieutenant, pointing out to the major a noisy fellow who was doing his best to excite the others, inquired whether he should 'blow his brains out'. 'Not just yet,' replied the major, quietly. All is well that ends well. Today, as the day before yesterday, the time of drill passed by without disturbance. The major looks calm and confident; it may be supposed that he does not quite say all that is in his mind.

Thursday, 8 September

The storm which we felt must be brewing has burst upon us today. At one o'clock p.m. we were suddenly informed that the lieutenant-colonel commanding the 30th Régiment de Marche was coming to review the battalion.

After passing through the ranks amidst profound silence, he congratulated the battalion on its orderly appearance. He then called out the ringleaders of Monday and Wednesday, reprimanded them severely, and sent off two of them to prison. He gave orders that the first and third companies should go the next day to keep guard at Sourdeval, and the sixth and seventh at Saint-Hilaire. In the evening he invited all the officers to a bowl of 'punch'; he spoke a kind word to each of them, and they went away well pleased with him.

Sourdeval, Friday, 9 September

The companies that had been ordered to change quarters started at seven; the others went for a training march to the town of Barenton. It has been pouring with rain the whole morning. Sourdeval-la-Barre is a pretty provincial town, half-way between Mortain and Vire, in the midst of a cluster of hills, amongst which is said to be the highest peak in Normandy. The townspeople are very hospitable, and vie with each other in regaling the Mobiles. There is a rumour that we are to be sent to Rennes.

Monday, 12 September

We hear that tomorrow morning the whole battalion is to start for Cherbourg. The two companies now quartered at Saint-Hilaire will sleep tonight at Mortain.

Tuesday, 13 September

We are in the train, rumbling along towards Cherbourg. This morning, for the first time, the whole battalion started together. We marched from Sourdeval to the station at Vire; the distance is four leagues. The men have as yet received nothing but forage-caps and some bad linen blouses. In the absence of knapsacks they have to carry their bundle as they can; but we hope to be supplied with all we want when we get to Cherbourg. The inhabitants of Mortain, Sourdeval, and Vire bade us farewell with heartfelt kindness, and their town bands followed us with very tolerable music.

The country we passed through is picturesque and hilly. The weather was splendid, with a blazing sun; the men sang all the way at the top of their voices. Notwithstanding our poor accoutrements, we looked brave enough. In front rode the major, erect and defiant, on his black charger; Adjutant-Major de Gerval: and Dr Bidard, our head surgeon, who has voluntarily left his practice to attend our sick and wounded. He is considered very skilful. Then followed all the companies. I have made friends already in many of them; I shall always rejoice to have known Christian de Failly, 'a mighty hunter' and a determined soldier, who commands the first. I am also much attached to my captain, Viallet. Quite in the rear, heading the lads from Teilleul, marches the best of men and of friends [Fernand de Rougé]. His countenance makes one think of the Sire de Joinville; like St Louis's companion, devoted to his family and his home, and casting at times a loving look behind, but as valiant as the old warrior, and no less faithful to his duty.

Cherbourg, Wednesday, 14 September

We arrived here at noon, after a very slow journey and a whole night spent in the train. The colonel in command of the place reviewed the battalion on the platform, after which we were sent off to our respective quarters. Our next move, it seems, will be to Carentan.

Friday, 16 September

Nothing new in our position. The life we lead here is not unpleasant. We drill from eight till ten, and from two till four. The rest of the day is pretty nearly at our own disposal. We go on the sea, and we pay visits to the ironclad fleet, now in the roadstead, under Admiral Rozé. We often go the 'Café de l'Europe', which is the rendezvous also of the officers from Avranches and Saint-Lô; for the three battalions of the 30th Régiment de Marche are now together. M. de Clinchamp commands Avranches, M. de Vains, Saint-Lô, and the whole is under the superior orders of Colonel Desmares, who has also come to take up his quarters in Cherbourg. These first days of autumn are magnificent. No particular news from the seat of war.

Thursday, 22 September

Nothing has been thought of since we have been here but the elections of the Garde Mobile officers, decreed by the Government of National Defence.[1]

It was believed at first that this process would be carried on all over France; then it was said that it would be confined to Paris alone. It seems that there was some hesitation here, and that Admiral Rozé and General Suhau, commandant of the town, did not consider themselves absolutely bound to obey the orders of the administration. However, the prefect appears to have carried the day.

At three o'clock the major arrived unexpectedly, while we were at drill, and gave us his orders respecting the elections, which are to take place tomorrow in the great court-yard of the barracks at Val-de-Serre.

Saturday, 24 September

The elections took place yesterday morning. Almost all the officers appointed by the Imperial Government were at once con-

---

[1] The decree of 16 September for the election of officers by the men themselves was an attempt by the Government to increase the officer strength of the Garde Mobile and to replace certain officers who had been removed for being too much attached to the Imperial regime. The results were generally unsatisfactory. Some of the officers relieved from their posts by the government were re-elected. Some of the elections were decided by bribery. In other cases, efficient officers with a sense of discipline were replaced by easy-going individuals who were popular with the men. The system remained in force to replace casualties and vacancies arising from other causes until repealed in December. The elections caused particular damage to efficiency and morale amongst the Paris group of the Garde Mobile, whose choice was always more capricious than that of the provinces.

firmed in their rank by the unanimous vote of their subordinates. Then the captains, lieutenants, and sub-lieutenants had to elect their major. There was no division of opinion; M. de Grainville secured all the votes; his devotion to his duty, his experience, his kindness to every one, and perhaps we must confess also his handsome countenance and his long black moustache, have won all hearts. . . .

Now that the elections are over, we are to be dismissed from our Capua. Tomorrow morning, at five, we start for Sottevast, a village some leagues hence towards Valognes and Carentan, where we are to encamp. We have spent this afternoon at Querqueville fort, receiving our camp equipages, tents, rugs, cans, and kettles; but still no knap-sacks. We shall leave Cherbourg imperfectly equipped, badly armed, and deplorably clothed. The jackets, trousers, and shoes which have been given us are of the worst description. We have sword-belts and cartridge-boxes; but they positively refuse to let us have *chassepots*. The real reason is, I imagine, that there are none; but the authorities wish us to believe that the old muskets are left to us because they are the best, and that if they had the new ones our Mobiles would spend all their cartridges in a quarter of an hour.[1] It seems to me that the inexperience of the Mobiles is a very good reason why they should be taught to be careful of their ammunition, but not why they should be supplied with inferior muskets, which, if they possess the singular merit of not being quickly loaded, have some very serious disadvantages. Perhaps we shall be told tomorrow that we may consider ourselves fortunate in having muskets of a short range, as our Mobiles will then be in less danger of causing accidents by their awkwardness. Nothing is more irritating than to be treated in this way like children, when those who are charged with the care of us are themselves so unequal to their task.

Sottevast Camp, Sunday, 25 September

Cotentin is a very pretty country. The valley of Sottevast is sheltered by rocky hills and curtained by woods. The meadow in which we are encamped belongs to M. de Chivray, whose picturesque old castle is hidden in the groves, a quarter of a mile off, on the banks of a clear stream called the Douve. The camp at this moment presents

---

[1] This is not altogether fanciful. The quick-loading and long range of the *chassepot* had led to a prodigious waste of ammunition, even amongst the regular soldiers.

a scene of grotesque illumination, which reminds me of Châlons. The Mobiles are settling down in their new life. They are gradually turning into soldiers; and as they are by trade butchers, tinmen, carpenters, or 'navvies', all sorts of workshops have been extemporised; and they will even in this wild district be able to supply all their wants. Down there, by the hillside, sheep are being slaughtered as in the days of Homer. At the entrance of the road, pork butchers and liquor vendors have established their stalls. We are quite ignorant as to the length of time we are to stay here. For the present, the officers are enjoying the kindest hospitality in the houses of MM. de Chivray and du Plessis de Grenédan.

We have left the depôt company at Cherbourg, in command of Captain Launay. The seven war companies are permanently organised, and number 171 men in each.

Wednesday evening, 28 September

We went today on a route march to Valognes. It is a quaint little town in the midst of lovely groves; the road which leads to it passes through several deep and secluded valleys, deliciously green and cool. Nearly the whole way is thickly shaded with trees. This excursion was a real party of pleasure. But on our return to Sottevast we learnt that we were to leave this paradise tomorrow, to go into quarters in some villages near the Carentan marshes. We shall thus be broken up into several detachments. I doubt whether we shall gain by these changes. What is certain is that we shall not be able to camp out long in this late season without running the risk of being decimated by sickness. We are living in a state of constant uncertainy: who can tell what the future has in store for us? The war is dragging on, the Germans are gaining ground, and some days ago they took possession of Mantes. Shall we succeed in ridding ourselves of these hordes? But these are not questions to be discussed at night, when there is a long journey before us on the morrow.

Pont-Labbé, Picauville, Monday, 3 October

We have been here since 29 September. In three-quarters of an hour the train conveyed us from Sottevast to the station at Chef-du-Pont, where the battalion divided; the second and sixth companies were sent to Sainte-Mère-Église, the fourth to Blosville, and the fifth remained at Chef-du-Pont; the first, the third, and the seventh came to Pont-Labbé Picauville, which is six kilometres from the station. It was a fair-day; the long wide street which forms the village was full of life and bustle; on the flights of stone steps which adorn almost every doorway were laid out every kind of merchandise, amongst which immense masses of butter were the most conspicuous articles. The houses of Pont-Labbé are several stories high, and very well built; but they are mostly thatched, which gives them a singular and picturesque appearance. The village stretches half-way up the hill, along the road which leads from Carentan to Saint-Sauveur le Vicomte, and is backed on the north by a grassy and fertile plain, crossed by the Valognes road. On the south side, by penetrating into the gardens behind the houses, you get a very striking view of the valley below. Those smooth meadows lying in the hollow, watered by a meandering stream, are converted in the winter into salt marshes, from the water of the bay of Carentan, which comes flowing up into the Douve. As there is some fear that we may be surprised here by the Prussians, every effort has been made to hasten the inundation;[1] and already, in more than one place, the river is turned into a lake ruffled by the sea-breeze, and with thousands of long-winged insects—offspring of the marshes—humming on its banks. To the right and left the river crawls among the poplars till it is lost to sight by the turning of the valley. Opposite to us rises a wooded eminence, over which the road descends to Prétot and Lessay, between immense brick-coloured banks. Till it reaches the foot of the hill it is a raised causeway, branching off from the high road at the end of the village, and crossing the marshes. Wide trenches have been dug in it, and at some points there is only a narrow strip left, just broad enough for one carriage; so that it would easily, in case of necessity, be cut through by a few strokes of the spade. The bridge over the river, they say, is mined; at all events, the holes are all ready. All this looks like apprehension. And yet it seems difficult to believe that the enemy would suddenly venture so far from their base of operations. I do not think the two batteries now being placed will have any great service to perform. However that may be, this is the post we have to defend; it seems we are to be here for some time. The men are billeted on the villages of Pont-Labbé and Picauville, which stand close together. They regret Mortain, Sourde-val, and even Cherbourg, where the people were not very open-

1 Similar action was taken by the German defenders of Normandy in 1943–44.

handed. Their right to fire and candle is not of much use to them, in a place where there is hardly such a thing as a fire or a candle to be found. Some of them are quartered at Bon-Sauveur, a large madhouse at the entrance of the village, where the credulous believe the Empress Charlotte[1] to be confined. The good nuns take all the care of the soldiers they can. The officers are lodged in a noisy, disorderly inn, the 'Cheval Blanc'. We have drill morning and evening; five hours a day in all. An order for target-shooting has been issued. We had begun while at Cherbourg to practise with powder.

Wednesday, 5 October

We began our target-shooting today, and it is to be continued tomorrow. A great number of our Mobiles have been sportsmen, and take a much better aim than one would expect. Our muskets are detestable, and it is aggravating to hear them spoken of as being so excellent. As we cannot be convinced on this point, they talk of giving us others. It looks as if they were trying to amuse us; if so, the attempt is not very successful.

Monday, 10 October

The weather is getting bad, and the marshes are beginning to fill with water. During the early part of the day we are left to ourselves. From twelve till five we drill; then we dine together, and do not separate till bedtime—a very unintellectual life, which will perhaps go on all winter.

Friday, 14 October

We are taking root in this country. It is cold now, and torrents of rain fall several times a day. The water is rising rapidly in the marshes, the roads are almost all flooded, and the country is gradually becoming impassable. For the last few days we have had with us a

[1] Wife of Maximilian of Austria who had been sent by Napoleon III as Emperor of Mexico and had been executed by firing squad, on the orders of the rebel leader. His wife as a result became insane. The commander of the French forces in Mexico had been Marshal Bazaine.

detachment of marine infantry; these béret-wearers are mounting guard with great pride before some old guns cast in the reign of Louis-Philippe, which have been placed in battery on the hill. There is no longer any idea of the Germans attacking us; but we are erecting huts, nevertheless, as though we were to spend the winter here. Rear-Admiral Jauréguiberry, who is in command of all the Cotentin troops, has appeared for a moment at Pont-Labbé. He pronounced a eulogium on muzzle-loaders, and led us to expect that we should not change our quarters for some time. These plains, swept by the four winds of heaven, will not be an agreeable residence when the cold season has set in, and the valleys are full of water, and all the roads are broken up.

In the meantime, till we know what our fate is to be, we diligently practise light infantry drill amongst the hedges and ditches with which the region abounds.

My new friend, Christian de Failly, has got four days' leave of absence. He has been ill for some time, and yet has persisted in performing all his duties. What a loss it would be if he had to leave us! From what I know of him, he will go on till he drops.

Tuesday, 18 October

Nothing new, except that we went this morning to pay the last military honours to a Mobile of the Isigny company, who has died of brain fever. He was buried in the church at Picauville. He is the first man we have lost.

The period of march and counter march which now faced the 30th Regiment was undoubtedly connected with some definite and also probably some imaginary enemy movements. After their encounter with 15 Corps on 10 October, the Bavarian Corps had occupied Orleans. The Prussian troops who had been with them, consisting of one infantry and one cavalry division under General von Wittlich, had been ordered to disperse the French volunteers assembling at Châteaudun and Chartres. On 24 October it took them twenty-four hours of murderous street fighting to clear Châteaudun, which was ably defeated by 1,200 franc-tireurs, supported by National Guard and inhabitants. As a punishment, the town was pillaged and burnt. As a result, when von Wittlich appeared outside Chartres three days later, the town surrendered immediately even though garrisoned by 7,000 irregulars and two

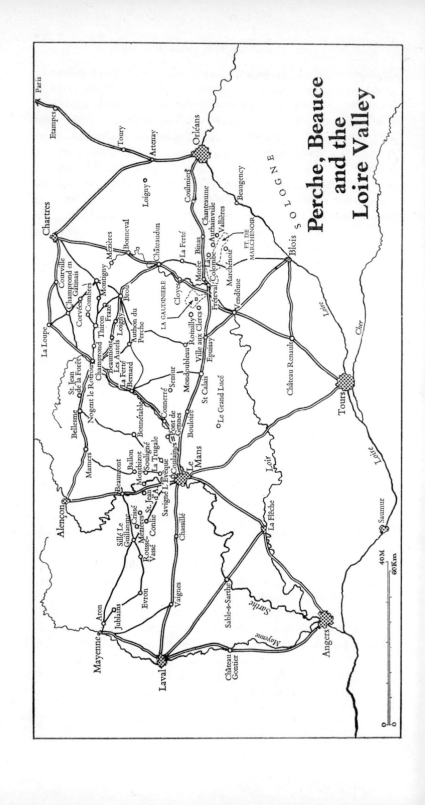

Perche, Beauce and the Loire Valley

Paris
Étampes
Toury
Artenay
Orléans
S O L O G N E
Chartres
Loigny
Coulmiers
Beaugency
Blois
Bonneval
Châteaudun
La Ferté
Binas
Morée
Chanteaume
Authainville
Vallières
FT. DE MARCHENOIR
Cloyes
Fréteval Colombe
Marchenoir
Vendôme
Courville
Champrond en Gâtinais
Mézières
Montigny
Frazé
Brou
LA GAUDINIERE
La Loupe
Corvées
Combres
Thiron
Beaumont
Les Autels Loigny
Champrond
La Ferté Bernard
Authon du Perche
Roinilly
Ville aux Clercs
St Jean de la Forêt
Bellesme
Nogent le Rotrou
Semur
Connerré
Pont de Gennes
Mondoublcau
Épuisay
Château Renault
Mamers
Bonnétable
Les Autels
La Trugale
St Calais
Le Grand Lucé
Cher
Beaumont
Ballon
Montbizot
Souligné
Savigné L'Évêque
Coulaines
Le Mans
Bouloire
Loir
Tours
Loire
Alençon
Sillé Le Guillaume
Crissé
Mézangers
Rousse-Vassé
Conlie
St Jean d'A.
Chassillé
La Flèche
Saumur
Aron
Jublains
Évron
Vaiges
Sablé-s-Sarthe
Sarthe
Angers
Mayenne
Château Gontier
Laval
Mayenne

40 M
60 Km

companies of marines. The Prussian troops were ordered to remain there. It was almost certainly the operation of their cavalry patrols to the west which kept Roger de Mauni's battalion on the move.

Caen, Hotel d'Angleterre, Tuesday, 25 evening

Yesterday, about twelve o'clock, arrived, quite suddenly, an order for our immediate departure. At two o'clock the battalion was on its way to Chef-du-Pont, where we were to take the train for Alençon. When we arrived nothing was ready, and no train available till the next morning. The men's patience and good humour were put to a severe trial. They had to encamp, at nightfall, in a wet meadow. Nothing is equal to the improvidence of the superior administration. In this wretched hamlet of Chef-du-Pont, the 3,500 men of the 30th Regiment were not able to procure more than a few pounds of bread amongst them, and scarcely any straw to lay over the mud in their tents. In our present circumstances hardships are doubly trying, from the consciousness that they are owing to the incapacity or the neglect of the staff officers; nothing makes one more indignant than to feel that with a little care and forethought the sufferings of some thousands of men might have been avoided.

This morning we spent two hours at the railway station, receiving a supply of cartridges, each man getting fifty for his share. Undoubtedly, we are being led to the front since we are entrusted for the first time with ammunition. We strive in vain to set the example of cheerfulness and gaiety; the men droop their heads beneath the rain which is falling in torrents—they feel that the good times are over, and that misery is beginning.

At eleven we started for Caen. After waiting three hours at the terminus the *billets de logement*[1] were given out, and the companies ordered to assemble at eight o'clock tomorrow in a square in the centre of the town. We have no idea what our destination is to be. I hear it said that we shall remain here for some days.

We ought to be in good spirits, since we may soon expect now to see the Prussians—an event we have so ardently desired.[2] And yet I feel oppressed with sadness. This cold, rainy weather is dispiriting . . . and then, nothing is so trying as to have to leave a place on the

[1] Billeting tickets.

[2] One of Victor Hugo's great cries was his desire to 'eat a few Prussians'.

sudden, even though one has been in it only as a sojourner. We had already made friends in our new quarters. I still have before my eyes the melancholy scene of our departure: the companies emerging from the market-place, where they had been cantoned, into the street; the sergeant-majors calling the roll, and the stragglers hastening to rejoin their ranks; at last the whole column setting itself in motion at the voice of the major, and a few paces behind Mesdames de Grainville and de Rougé, sad yet calm, watching our battalion as it moved away. We are sometimes told that these emotions are enervating and depressing. I think they tend rather to make one serious.

Last night, at Chef-du-Pont, we saw a great Aurora Borealis, that seemed to set the sky on fire. Today we have seen it again. Would the ancients have taken it for a good or a bad omen?

Luigny, near Nogent-Le-Rotrou Friday, 28 October

We came here last night. What for? I have no idea, nor have any of my friends. This is not to be wondered at; but I fear that the ignorance on this important point is universal.

Luigny is an ugly, straggling town, on the high-road from Nogent to Brou, on the last slopes of the hills of Perche. Looking out of the window of the little cottage in which I am writing, I see towards the south the road to Châteaudun winding over undulating plains; there, three leagues off, is Chapelle-Royale, where the Avranches battalion is encamped. Immediately behind the house rises a barren hill; the way up to it is the road to Frazé, a little village two leagues to the north, where the battalion of the Sarthe is quartered.

We had a wearisome journey from Caen. Our orders were issued from so great a distance, and from heights so far above us, that neither our colonel nor our major could make anything of them. We had best say at once that we have no orders at all, and that we are left entirely to chance.

We left Caen at six in the morning. After the eight o'clock muster the men were dismissed, and we had our orders for two o'clock. At twelve the officers were informed that we were to start immediately, and that the men must be sent direct to the station, wherever they might be found. Under such circumstances our departure was attended with a certain amount of confusion, and it was impossible to ascertain the exact number of the effectives. When we had passed the Argentan station we began to hear of the Prussians; at Séez they were declared to be close at hand, and we were recommended to place some of our men on the engine with their muskets loaded. Nothing came of it, however, and no extreme measures were resorted to.

When we arrived at the Alençon station we were suddenly told that we were going on to Le Mans; new instructions, it was said, had been transmitted verbally to Colonel Desmares through the station master. From Mans we pushed on to Nogent-le-Rotou, on similar authority; it was becoming evident that the war was going to be carried out at random.

Colonel Rousseau, who is in command at Nogent, and receives his orders from General Fierrec, is said to have been greatly astonished yesterday morning, at six o'clock, when a train of interminable length deposited on the platform 1,200 wearied Mobiles, badly equipped, badly armed, badly clothed. When explanations were given, it was agreed that such a reinforcement could only have come direct from Providence; for just then a position had to be guarded five leagues off, and we were sent to it on the instant.

There was a distribution of gaiters, and a few shirts and trousers; and then we ascended the hill of Nogent, and began our march of twenty kilometres through a flat and frightful country, in dark rainy weather.

The men, already very much fatigued, had to carry their things in wretched canvas bags, the straps of which cut their shoulders. Night was falling as we entered Luigny. No quarters having been prepared, the troops had to encamp in a muddy field exposed to the east wind, and every moment deluged with rain. The sight of the camp, when morning began to dawn, was pitiable. The officers were amazed at the patience and fortitude of the soldiers.

Saturday, 29 October

Nothing new in our situation. Yesterday we thought we should have rested; but the enemy being reported in the direction of Brou, the battalion was sent there to reconnoitre. Several times on the way we fancied we saw the Uhlans. We were mistaken; but the Uhlan is in the air—one has only to hear how the peasants talk about them.

We reached Brou without having seen anything, and the battalion was quietly drawn up in the market-place. Then the major went to the town-hall, where he was given to understand by the chief magistrate that the citizens of Brou had no intention of defending themselves.

The major was confounded by this frank declaration, and thought to himself that the citizens of Brou had little inclination for heroism. But when he found that in one of the rooms at the town-hall 600 pounds of bread lay secreted, his indignation knew no bounds, and he loaded the mayor with the most vehement reproaches. It was evident that these stores were not intended for us, since French troops were neither expected nor desired in the town. But then, for whom were they destined? It was difficult to say. The mayor assumed a dignified attitude. 'You do not know me!' he cried, with a theatrical air. 'And I have not the slightest desire to know you,' replied M. de Grainville, casting upon him a look of the most supreme contempt. He then remounted his horse, and we returned as we came, disgusted with the selfishness and cowardice we had witnessed.

It seems that during the colloquy with the mayor twelve German horsemen were quietly supping in a farm-house 500 yards from the town. In such cases the country people are very careful not to give the alarm, knowing that the enemy would return in force if they did so, and burn down their houses.

Having got back to Luigny, we lodged our men in the granaries and in the church. The first and the fourth companies are on outpost duty at Perruchet and Dampierre, villages between Luigny and Brou. Five hundred Uhlans are said to be at this moment amusing themselves in Brou: much good may it do them!

Today we are left in peace. The colonel, who lodges close by, at the château of General Lebreton, has just reviewed the battalion; he complimented us on our good appearance. His conduct towards us since the elections at Cherbourg shows that he knows how to forgive; he is said to know a good many other things besides.

It has become bitterly cold; during the review we were half frozen. If our men are not supplied with better clothing their sufferings will be very great.

We hear that the Prussians have fallen back a few leagues; can it be at our approach? All the reports circulated as to the movements of the enemy appear to me to be entirely without foundation.

Luigny, Monday, 23 October, evening

Yesterday we went on a routine march as far as Frazé, a village hidden in a little valley embosomed in forests, and flanked by a fine old castle. The men of Sarthes, who are stationed there, exhibited their *chassepots* with great pride; our Mobiles, who have only the old muskets, believe themselves to be foresaken by God and man. This deficiency in the supply of arms is deplorable; it is time we should protest against it in earnest.

This morning ten Chasseurs d'Afrique arrived, well equipped and splendidly mounted, and with mousqueton *chassepots*. We are told they are to act as scouts. Up to this moment we have not had a single horseman, to communicate with the other companies, or to make any reconnoitring movements during our marches. Yet there is nothing we are more in want of than some connecting link between all these detachments of Mobiles, scattered over a distance of twenty leagues, between Nogent and Châteaudun, without artillery or cavalry. The commanding officers are left in great measure without any precise orders or instructions. I can find no one to tell me what we are doing here. What is certain is, that we have not been able to prevent the Prussians from entering Châteaudun, a week ago, and turning everything into fire and blood.[1]

Today, for a change, we went to Brou. We saw nothing there but the face, already familiar to us, of M. Le Maire. But, to make amends, we had the satisfaction of marching six leagues; for the last two days, however, we have had knapsacks, which greatly lessens our fatigue.

Luigny, Wednesday, 2 November

Yesterday, three companies, of which mine was one, were sent again to Brou. We were told we were to stay there to protect the next day's market, and to support, if necessary, a body of troops that are marching upon Illiers. We, therefore, began to look out for quarters; the Mobiles were disposed of in the dancing-rooms and out-houses, and one detachment was sent to explore the environs, and establish the outposts; this gave me an immense walk, which was full of interest.

Brou is a sort of crossway, on the confines of Beauce and Perche. The roads to the south lead to Courtalain and Châteaudun; at four leagues' distance, to the east, is Bonneval, a small and ancient town, like Brou. The road which takes you to it from Brou passes through Yévres, a large village, the houses of which are scattered over the plain; the church tower, which is a great height, is occupied by the National

[1] This was General von Wittlich's action already referred to.

Guards, who please themselves by thinking that they are placed there to keep watch over the country. The landscape is flat and scantily wooded, except on the north-west, towards Frazé, where a corner of Perche comes in sight.

We should have been much better off at Brou than at Luigny, where there was nothing to assuage our hunger but emaciated turkeys, which our landlord threw head foremost into an indescribable sort of black broth, and then announced that 'dinner was served'. At Brou there is an excellent cook, who has made the fortune of the inn, 'Le Plat d'Etain'. There are grocers, tailors, watchmakers, gunsmiths, and even a bookseller, who sells maps of the country. But we were only allowed to have a glimpse of this land of promise. At ten o'clock in the evening a gendarme suddenly arrived, bringing an order for us to return to Luigny. We had hastily to recall our outposts, and set ourselves in motion again. We arrived at Luigny at one o'clock in the morning.

Today there are rumours of peace. Bazaine, they say, has made terms that would not be dishonourable . . . others accuse him of treachery. All this is confused, and, to my mind, forebodes nothing good.

Thursday, 3 November

It is fine, but the cold is invading us, and the days are getting short; the prospect of winter is an anxious one, in our present circumstances—the men are so ill-clothed, and, above all, so miserably shod. Many of them have their feet already in a pitiable condition.

But we ought to make no complaint today, for we are left in peace by our firesides. Captain Viallet is gone to Tours with a petition for *chassepots,* signed by all the officers of the battalion; if he returns successful, we shall soon forget our miseries. . . . I cannot say that the soldiers I see passing to and fro under my windows look particularly wretched. Excepting two or three, who are expiating their youthful follies in General Lebreton's pigeon-house (transformed into a police-station), they are all greatly enjoying the repose which has been granted to us.

Luigny, Saturday, 5 November

If Captain Viallet had not returned in triumph yesterday, with 1,200 *chassepots* and 80,000 cartridges, we should all have been in great despair this morning, for the capitulation of Metz is now an ascertained fact.[1] Gambetta in his proclamation, accuses Bazaine of being a traitor. 'A traitor!' no—but selfish and ambitious. He wished to spare his army, and remain, standing alone, arbitrator and ruler of the destinies of France after Paris had fallen. The resistance of France has upset his calculations, and he has passed through the 'Caudine forks' with 120,000 men, 500 guns, and fifty flags or standards.

The predominant sensation today in the battalion is that of fatigue. At Illiers, in Beauce, there is an old cavalry officer—and now a colonel of Mobiles—called M. de M. The night before last he sent to our Colonel Lemoine-Desmares for reinforcements. He wrote word that he was certain to be attacked the next morning, at six o'clock, by superior forces. M. de Grainville was his ancient comrade and friend; he knew that he could rely upon him; and on the men of Mortain. There was no time to lose, and every available man was turned out. We started immediately. It was midnight, and the cold was piercing. At Brou we had a rest of twenty minutes. Some of the men succeeded in rousing a baker and procuring a little bread, but the greater number remained on the pavement, standing behind their piled arms and huddling together to keep themselves from freezing. At four o'clock we were again on the road, pressing on to Vieuxvic. It was the first time we had marched all night; the men were dropping from fatigue, hunger, and want of sleep; but the hope of seeing the Prussians gave them energy, and they were making every exertion to reach their destination, when the news arrived that Colonel de M. had evacuated Illiers at four o'clock and that it was high time for us to retire, unless we wished to find ourselves in a serious predicament. Our disappointment was at its height. . . . What is to become of us if the last hopes of France are entrusted to such careless hands as these?

Although Colonel de M. had left us nothing to do but to think of our own safety, our major thought it advisable to push on to the end, that we might join the column which was evacuating Illiers, and sup-

[1] After the war Bazaine was tried and sentenced to death as a traitor, his sentence afterwards being reduced to life imprisonment. It is difficult to agree fully with the verdict of treachery. There may have been, at the back of his mind, a feeling that it would be better to keep his army intact as the last element of law and order in revolutionary France, rather than waste it in attempts to break out. He certainly entered into some negotiations with the enemy, which was a dangerous thing to do when his opponent had the acumen of Bismarck. But his final capitulation was forced upon him by shortage of food, and it was due only to sheer inefficiency that he had not introduced immediate rationing of all comestibles, and particularly salt, from the very beginning of the siege.

port it in case of need, or assist it in repulsing an attack. Colonel de M. had withdrawn into the hills, and was said to be at Montigny, a small village three leagues south-west of Illiers. In order to find him, we had to turn to the left, defiling almost under the walls of Illiers, and exposing our flank to the enemy, whose position we could not ascertain, having no cavalry. This difficult movement was executed without accidents, and we returned by Montigny and Frazé. It appears that Colonel de M. had forgotten us![1]

But we are now happy in the possession of good muskets, and proud at having accomplished thirteen leagues.

There is great talk of an armistice of twenty-five days, which is on the point of being concluded.

Luigny, Monday, 7 November evening

Since yesterday morning we have been practising very zealously with our *chassepots*; the old muskets have been sent back to Nogent. We hear that the negotiations for the armistice have been definitively broken off.

Some days ago Lieutenant Doynel was entrusted with a company of twenty-five picked men of the battalion, to go on a reconnoitring expedition, and give information of the enemy's movements. He has just returned from Illiers, bringing the major a sabre belonging to a Prussian lancer; they have killed two of the enemy, and severely wounded several; five of our men have not reappeared. This is the first encounter we have to register in the annals of our battalion. Colonel Lemoine-Desmares and the major congratulated Lieutenant Doynel on the bravery of which he had brought back such convincing proofs.

[1] Colonel de M.'s explanation is, that the Chasseur d'Afrique whom he sent with the letter requesting reinforcements, had brought back no answer signed by Colonel Desmares.

III

The Army of the West

These activities of General Fierrec's Army of the West which had appeared to Roger de Mauni, and doubtless to many others, to be largely aimless, had in fact served a very useful purpose. In the first place, they had distracted the enemy's attention from the formation of 16 Corps around Blois and in the second had given the Prussian High Command the false impression that the bulk of the French forces were concentrated at Le Mans. This mistake was to distort their thinking for some time to come.

The French plan, approved and energetically supported by Gambetta, was for the Army of the Loire under General d'Aurelle de Palandines to concentrate around Blois by the end of October, to wrest Orleans from General von der Tann's Bavarian Corps and to advance on Paris to link up with General Ducrot's expected break-out in early November. The timings for this plan had been upset by Bazaine's capitulation at Metz. The French forces should have moved forward to reach Orleans on 31 October, but on the 28th rumours from Metz had reached the Army of the Loire and d'Aurelle had hesitated. When on the 30th Bazaine's surrender was confirmed, it was more important than ever that the army should now move immediately if it was to achieve anything before the arrival on the scene of the besieging troops under Prince Frederick Charles. But now there were these rumours of an armistice, as noted by Roger de Mauni, and again d'Aurelle waited to see what would happen. Not until 7 November did the Army of the Loire advance.

General von der Tann had for some time felt that the attack would come down the Loire valley and that its objective would be Orleans. His feeling was not, however, shared by his superiors. On the evidence of von Wittlich's experience around Chartres and Châteaudun, and in accordance with the rumours that were reported to him from inside Paris, von Moltke considered that the real danger was in the west. For it was common knowledge within the capital that the direction of Ducrot's break-out would be along the lower Seine towards Rouen and the west. What von Moltke did not know was that Gambetta and Ducrot were, as a result of the difficulties of communication between Paris and the outside, each ignorant of the other's intention, and that Gambetta and the Army of the Loire expected that the link up with Ducrot would take place somewhere to the south of Paris.

To deal with the danger as he saw it, von Moltke decided on 7 November to form a powerful Army Detachment under the command of the Duke of Mecklenburg-Schwerin. This Detachment was to consist of the Bavarian Corps, two infantry divisions and two cavalry divisions and its task was 'To break up the Army of the Loire now in process of formation and to compel it to retreat by Le Mans. . . .' The Detachment by 12 November was to be formed up in the Chartres-Châteaudun area facing west, a small force being left in Orleans to protect the town. It was obvious that as a result of General Fierrec's activities and of correct, but misleading, information from Paris, von Moltke completely misappreciated the direction of the threat.

Von der Tann on the other hand was by 8 November certain that an attack on Orleans was imminent. To avoid being bottled up in the town he moved his troops during the night to a position in the open to the west of Orleans, his centre being based on the village of Coulmiers. His force amounted to 14,500 infantry, 4,500 cavalry and 120 guns. At 8 a.m. on 9 November he was attacked by 15 Corps and two divisions of 16 Corps, amounting in all to 72,000 infantry, 7,000 cavalry and 160 guns. By the evening the Bavarians were in retreat. By an error there were no French cavalry at hand to carry out the pursuit, and the third division of 16 Corps, which could have cut off the withdrawal, had not reached the field of battle. Nevertheless, the French had at last gained an indisputable victory.

On 10 November, when von der Tann's retreating Bavarians reached Toury to join the other forces which were forming the Duke of Mecklenburg's Detachment, it was expected that the French would continue the advance at any moment. The Duke was ordered to guard the road to Paris. For three days he awaited a French attack and for three days his cavalry patrols reported no enemy movements; when they reported that the French had even disappeared from around Orleans, he began to think that perhaps von Moltke had been right in the first instance and that the Army of the Loire had gone off to join the forces at Le Mans for an advance on Paris from the west.

On 13 November, therefore, he started to move with the main body towards Chartres, leaving only one cavalry division at Toury to guard the road.

But it was his patrols that were at fault. In fact, not one single French soldier had moved from around Orleans after the battle of Coulmiers. When Gambetta arrived on 12 November to congratulate the army on its victory, he found General d'Aurelle recommending an immediate withdrawal in view of the probability of a German counter attack which he would not be able to withstand. Gambetta, on the other hand, was for an immediate advance on Paris by the most direct route, even though there was no longer any evidence of an imminent break-out from within the city. Since the general stated flatly that this was impossible, it was decided to compromise and to fortify the Orleans district to serve as a firm base for an advance at a later date when more forces would be available. Three new Corps, 17, 18 and 19 were forming on the Loire and another, 21 Corps, at Le Mans. Even so, this pause, so necessary from the point of view of a conventionally trained soldier like d'Aurelle, was to prove a fatal mistake. For the moment the road to Paris lay virtually open. Prince Frederick Charles with the Second Army was making his way with all speed from Metz in the east, but his three Corps were well strung out and could not possibly concentrate north of Orleans before the 25th. The Duke of Mecklenburg had left only one cavalry division at Toury. Had the Army of the Loire, even with only two Corps, advanced at once, they must have broken through. There is no saying that they could have raised the siege, particularly as Ducrot was facing in the wrong direction to meet them with a break-out from within, but at least they would have temporarily outmanoeuvred thier opponents and have been moving towards the capital. As it was, to sit and do nothing could only give the Germans time to concentrate against them.

For over ten days the opportunity remained. During this time the Army of the West drew upon itself the whole weight of the Detachment, luring it to the west and away from the direct approach to Paris from Orleans. By 22 November, when the German High Command finally decided that the real danger lay at Orleans and not at Le Mans, the Army of the West had begun to disintegrate under the pressure. Roger de Mauni's diary of that fortnight reveals clearly the terrible demoralisation produced by lack of information and apparent loss of purpose. He bitterly attacks Gambetta for their suffering, though in reality what fault there was lay in the almost total inexperience of most intermediate levels of command and the failure of d'Aurelle de Paladines to take advantage of the situation which their sacrifice had created.

Roger de Mauni to His Sister

Luigny, 2 November 1870

My dear Louise,

We shall have been in this dismal place a week tomorrow. Men and officers arrived in a state of great fatigue. From Nogent-le-Rotrou to Luigny is five leagues. We got to Nogent at nine in the morning, and after a night passed in the train we were turned out into the mud, and there we had to draw up the men, who were hungry, weary, wet, miserable, and prevent them from dispersing whilst we went to get them food. After waiting a long time we were allowed to dismiss them for half an hour, and we ran to an inn to find a morsel for ourselves. At twelve the men were again assembled, and, after an hour's waiting, we started on foot for Luigny. When we had gone a league, Captain de Failly, who was in command of the vanguard, gave notice that two Prussian cuirassiers were in sight. We searched the woods, loaded our muskets, and looked about in all directions; but there was nothing to be seen, and we had no further alarm. We did not know exactly where the Prussians were. At this moment we are almost certain that they are at a distance of twenty kilometres. What made the march from Nogent to Luigny particularly arduous was that the men were laden with wallets that had been given out at Cherbourg, as a makeshift till the knapsacks were ready, which arrived only a few days ago. The canvas bands got twisted and cut their shoulders, and many had shoes which were either new or in bad condition, a most serious trouble, which we lament every day. And also, under the influence of the bad weather and fatigue, discontent, annoyance, and vexation were constantly on the increase, though they behaved in spite of everything with admirable patience.

We arrived at night, the men counting the moments that passed and every step they took. As no preparation had been made, we had to make them encamp in the midst of a muddy field, wet and worn out as they were, and then when they had pitched their tents they had to go in search of something to eat and a few wisps of straw to sleep on. It was heartrending. Our own fatigue is nothing; but when you have to urge on those from whom more is demanded than human strength can accomplish—when you have to enforce obedience at all costs, and speak sharply to a troop of brave and devoted men such as ours, you cannot help feeling your heart oppressed, however little your voice may show it.

The next day our men were installed in the church, where they are not very well off, but, at all events, they are sheltered from the rain which from time to time keeps falling in torrents. We have not many sick, but many have their feet cut to pieces by these last marches, and rest is an absolute necessity for them. For myself, I am wonderfully well able to withstand fatigue. I am very well shod, and I am in perfect health. The soldiers are almost always sure to be at the end of their strength before I am; but those who have the misfortune to be small and weakly suffer greatly.

Brou, Thursday, 10 November

The day before yesterday we took our final leave of Luigny—that horrible place—to establish ourselves at Brou. Here we are in the first line, and, it must be confessed, in a very insecure position, for we have left the *bocage,* and are now far on in Beauce. We are, in consequence, taking all possible precautions.

We are barricading the town; whilst one set of Mobiles are learning to form the square, the others are transporting rafters and paving stones to the outlets of the roads leading to Châteaudun, Illiers, and Luigny. Every night forty men and one officer keep guard on the road to Bonneval and Châteaudun; and as many on the road to Illiers and Courtalain.

It is snowing and raining; our unhappy men are all in rags, thanks to the care of our council of administration; fortunately they have good nests of hay and straw in which to pass the night.

We still hear a great deal of the success of the French arms. A week ago a great victory was reported near Courville, three leagues north of Illiers; today the Prussians are evacuating Chartres.[1] . . . We must not quite believe all this.

The five men who were left behind at Illiers on Monday, and who were supposed to be dead or taken prisoners, have all come back.

Brou, Friday, 11 November

This morning the weather is milder. We are going to pay the last honours to a Garde Mobile of the first company, who has just died in the hospital. He had lost his way, whilst acting as flanker on a night march, and having been perceived by the men of the battalion, and not answering to the 'Qui vive!' three times repeated, he was shot close to the muzzle.

Brou, Saturday, 12 November

The cold has returned; we have just sent a petition to Saint-Lô for winter clothing.

There is not much patriotism to be found in this district; the towns-people lose no opportunity of being insolent. As to the peasants, they find it very profitable to take their cattle to the Prussian camp, where they get a good price for them; and if it was not for their fear of getting shot, they would do so with the greatest alacrity. Captain Viallet acts as commandant of the place, and nothing enters or leaves Brou without a pass signed by him.

The lieutenant-colonel came today to inspect our barricades, and he expressed approval.

It is now a certain fact that General d'Aurelle de Paladines has gained a victory at Orleans; the moral effect, as they say, produced by this news is excellent.[2]

Brou, Wednesday, 16 November

It has been less cold these three last days, which is a great relief.

The market place presented this morning a most picturesque appearance. A hundred and fifty horsemen, lancers and dragoons were

[1] Von Wittlich's forces in fact remained at Chartres, using it for a base for their further advance to the west.

[2] The victory at Coulmiers.

drawn up in good order, the officers calling the roll. They had arrived from Mans under the command of General Guépratte. I gazed with respectful sadness on these relics of the splendid regiments destroyed at Reichshoffen and Sedan, which were once the pride of our country and the admiration of strangers. By ten o'clock men, horses, and carriages had all disappeared—they were already far on upon their way to Châteaudun.

Yesterday and the day before the major sent parties of scouts to Bonneval,[1] where the Prussians were expected to appear in great force. I conducted one of these expeditions. We saw nothing. The only thing I could do was to make inquiries of a wounded German, but he gave no information of any consequence.

Brou, Thursday, 17 November, evening

We are advancing: tomorrow morning the whole battalion is to occupy Mézières-au-Perche, a small village two miles to the north-east, between the Illiers and Bonneval roads. The stations of Dampierre and Perruchet, which have been up to this time held by the first and fifth companies, are to be abandoned; the fourth company, left at Luigny, will also join us.

Illiers, Saturday, 19 November, evening

We arrived at Mézières yesterday at eleven o'clock and we were breakfasting in one of those large farmhouses which are the pride of Beauce, when our major suddenly received orders to march to Champrond, to place himself at the disposal of Colonel Rousseau. Champrond-en-Gastine is a town eight leagues north-west of Mézières, on the road which leads from Nogent to Chartres, through La Loupe and Courville. It was sharp work, but we set forth again very courageously. Illiers, where we had been a fortnight before, lay on our way. We were within half a league of the town when we heard several cannon shots very close to us, and we saw the smoke of the conflagrations lighted by the enemy in the surburbs on the Chartres road. At the same moment we perceived that a battalion of Mobiles had taken up their position on the heights, evidently in expectation of the enemy.

[1] On the Chartres–Châteaudun road.

The major ordered us immediately to turn to the left, and conceal ourselves under the steep banks of a stream that ran by the wayside, and formed a natural entrenchment. At the same time scouts were sent on to explore the road. We soon learnt that Illiers was occupied by the French and menaced by the Prussians. The major instantly resolved on marching forward to the town, to offer Colonel de M. the support of his troops, and we started at the most rapid pace. A quarter of an hour afterwards we were drawn up in the crooked streets of the little Beauceronne city. The German firing had ceased, but several houses at the end of the town were in flames. Colonel de M. expecting to be attacked again the next day, requested M. de Grainville to remain. It was getting late, the Mortain men were famished and exhausted; and, besides, in the instructions given to the commanding officers night marches were prohibited. The major decided, therefore, to stay, and a dispatch was sent to Colonel Rousseau, at Champrond, for further orders. The answer was that the battalion of Mortain had been sent to headquarters because troops were wanted that could be relied upon, but that Illiers being threatened, we were to remain there to defend the town. It is vexatious that Captain de Failly has not been able to hear of our altered movements; he is escorting the baggage with his company, and had to take a separate road, as the one we followed was impracticable for wheeled vehicles; no doubt he has gone on to Champrond.

The battalion was quartered, as well as it could be, in the houses at Illiers; two companies are on guard at the château of La Folie, on the hill towards Brou. Today some of our detachments went out towards Chartres, and spent the whole afternoon in an unsuccessful chase after Uhlans. I descried from the top of the church-tower, riding over the plain at the distance of a quarter of a league, the first Prussians it has been my good fortune to see. Whenever the enemy is in sight the great bell tolls three times to give warning; we heard this ominous sound this morning, but there was no serious alarm. From my high observatory I could see a great way. Chartres is eight leagues off, and on a clear day the towers of the cathedral are distinctly visible.

Le Mans, 24 November

Those amongst us who live the longest will remember to their latest day the events in which we have just been engaged, either as actors or spectators.

On Sunday, 20 November at 8 a.m., the bell of the church at Illiers tolled three times. I left the house where I was lodging to rejoin my company. The faces of the officers I met on the way betrayed the deepest anxiety. When I reached the Place de l'Église I saw the major on horseback. He told me we were to retreat into Perche, and make our first halt at Montigny. Colonel de M. had received orders to that effect from General Rousseau. The dispatch had arrived during the night, and bad news had come at the same time. The battalion of Saint-Lô had been surprised and overpowered at Corvées; other corps had been driven back towards La Loupe; the Germans had suddenly advanced in overwhelming numbers from all sides, and resistance had been useless.

At nine o'clock we set out again sorrowfully upon our march. For a moment we had believed that we were going to the front in earnest; the localities in the neighbourhood of Luigny and Brou had seemed to us definitively wrested from the Prussians, and we could not think without a bitter sense of humiliation that the whole of this part of the country was thus to be given back into their hands.

The column then leaving Illiers comprised, besides the battalion of Mortain, two battalions of the Orne Mobiles and one of Calvados, making altogether about 4,000 men.

The tavern keepers at Illiers, after having well fleeced us during those two days, watched our departure with an air of great satisfaction, calculating that they would soon be dispensing their poisons to the Germans, without having been plundered—a misfortune they could not have escaped if the town had been defended by force of arms. Some of them even began to ridicule and jeer at us; but their taunts passed by unheeded.

Montigny, where we spent the afternoon of that day and part of the following night, is a village three leagues and a half from Illiers, on the road to Frazé and Luigny, which winds over hill and dale, crossing this part of Perche from the north-west to the south-east. We found there a few horsemen and two or three well-mounted field-pieces, that were to be added to our column.

The village was destitute of everything; it was in vain to look for a morsel of bread or a bundle of straw, or a dry corner under a roof. After the distribution of a few trousers and pairs of shoes, of which we were in the most urgent need, part of the troops had to encamp, and the rest were crammed into the cottages. In the meantime the most alarming reports were flying about, and many of the officers declared that if we stayed where we were, we should be cut off by the Prussians. I knew not what to think from all I heard; I only felt that an awful anxiety—the precursor of some great catastrophe—had fallen upon all of us, from the highest officer down to the lowest soldier, and I knew that so general a presentiment could scarcely be without foundation. We had no precise intelligence; but it was certain that the enemy had appeared in great force towards Senonches, and that it had been found impossible to check their progress through the forests which surrounded the town. In all probability, therefore, they were actually masters of La Loupe, and nearer to Nogent than to us.[1]

Towards evening some accurate information was received by Colonel de M. General Rousseau sent him word that he was compelled to evacuate Champrond in haste, and that a general retrograde movement was necessary.

In spending the whole day at Montigny, notwithstanding the danger incurred, Colonel de M. had acted according to his instructions; but after the dispatch from headquarters, every moment's delay became unpardonable. The men were not fatigued, and would have been glad enough to leave their detestable quarters as soon as possible; besides, there was no longer any object in avoiding night marches, and the darkness would have favoured our retreat. It is, therefore, difficult to explain why Colonel de M. never gave the order to march till four in the morning. He only sent Léonce Josset, sub-lieutenant of the battalion of Mortain, before us to inform M. Candau, who was in command of a battalion of Mobiles of the Loire-Inférieure, that he was to march to Thiron, a village half-way between Montigny and Nogent. M. Josset was at the same time to order MM. de Clinchamp and de Vains, in command of the men of Avranches and Saint-Lô, to concentrate their forces at Thiron, where the column from Illiers was to arrive early in the morning. A body of six or seven thousand men could thus have been assembled. MM. de Vains and de Clinchamp were not under Colonel de M., and, as they thought it prudent to retire in all haste, they marched towards Bellesme without attending to his orders. It would be an act of presumption to blame them for having done so.

M. Josset came back when the night was far advanced; and on hearing the discouraging intelligence he brought, the colonel decided on immediately striking the camp. Our departure was effected with

[1] The main enemy advance was, in fact, from Chartres along the road to Nogent-le-Rotrou.

as little noise as possible, and in the midst of the most profound darkness. By eight o'clock we had marched fourteen kilometres. A beautiful autumn day was dawning as we entered the principal street of Thiron; there we halted, and the companies drew up in a line along the pavement.

Captain de Failly, who had arrived from Champrond just in time to join us, had heard all the various reports that had been in circulation that morning and the day before. He asserted, with the authority of one who knows and understands what he is saying, that we should run the greatest risk of being surrounded unless we continued to retreat with the utmost speed.

Nothing could be more true. Whilst we were halting at Thiron the Germans were advancing on our right,[1] beyond the little town of La Loupe and the village of Combres; on the left,[2] they were overrunning Brou and the country about Luigny and Beamont-les-Autels.

But Colonel de M. was of another opinion. In spite of the representations addressed to him by several officers, he gave orders that we were to remain for the present at Thiron; the battalion of Mortain, having encamped the day before, was to be cantoned in the houses, and one of the four others was to supply the outposts. Major Candau and Major Boudonnet excused themselves, one after the other, from this duty, stating that their men were too weary. The colonel, provoked by their refusal, sent for the men of Mortain. They had neither eaten nor slept for twenty-four hours; nevertheless, their major felt that he could answer for them as he would for himself. We had, therefore, to turn our backs upon the town, expiring with hunger and thirst, and to climb a steep hill to the north, in order to pitch our tents half-way up. When we had reached our destination the battalion turned round, and we could survey the road by which we had come. Five hundred yards beneath us, at the foot of an abrupt descent, I could see, winding right and left, the road from Montigny to Nogent, which runs through the village, and then is lost amongst the wooded hills. By the roadside flows a little river, crossed by several small bridges. The valley is so narrow that on the other side of the road the mountain rises like a wall; clumps of trees intercept the view over the plain. The town of Thiron-Gardais, numbering about 1,500 inhabitants lies at the bottom of this funnel, embosomed in forests, which

[1] That is to the north.

[2] To the south.

are one or two thousand yards in depth. Our line of battle was perpendicular to the Combres road which emerges from the village, and ascends directly towards the north; it disappears on the right of camp, amongst the brushwood in the midst of which we were crouching.

Many of us who had heard what was said down below, looked anxiously around on all sides, straining our eyes in the endeavour to penetrate the depths of the woods, and to see what could be hidden within them. Suddenly, on the edge of a glade, on the opposite side of the valley, two horsemen came in sight, soon followed by several others. They put their horses to a gallop, and rapidly scoured the plain in every direction; but a few shots being sent after them from Thiron, they turned sharp round and disappeared behind the trees.

At that moment the third company went to take up an advanced post by the side of the road, a few hundred paces farther on, upon the road to Combres. Captain Viallet and his lieutenant were just coming out of a by-path, where they had been placing sentries, when they perceived, at the distance of sixty yards before them, a party of Uhlans cautiously advancing along the skirts of the wood. We fired upon them; they fled at full speed, and we went to give our major information of what we had seen.

M. de Grainville, having heard the firing, was just coming towards us. The companies were drawn up on the road; the Abbé de Longue-ville, a volunteer chaplain, who had joined us a week before, was pronouncing absolution; the soldiers were trying the hammers of their muskets—every one thought the hour was come.

But still we could neither hear nor see anything. The colonel had sent orders that the men should make their soup, and repitch the camp; the major, however, considered it prudent to send a company to reconnoitre the woods on the plain of Combres. The third was entrusted with this duty.

We started to the right, and returned in three-quarters of an hour by the high road, after having gone over a wide semicircle. We had seen nothing; but the country people declared that the Prussians were in great force at Combres, which is only six kilometres distant, and that they might be expected at any moment.

Colonel de M. now came up in his turn—gay, pleasant, elegant as always, and fortified by a good breakfast at Thiron. He lighted his cigar with the most charming self-possession, and assured us that we need not think we were in any imminent danger from the Prussians, since they 'never—never made an attack after eleven in the morning'.[1]

The major gave orders, notwithstanding, that the positions were to be maintained, and that no one should absent himself. I followed my captain to the post which was to be occupied by the third. It was a deep ravine on the left-hand side of the road, where a large body of men could easily lie in ambush. Scarcely were we installed there when fresh intelligence arrived, which left us no longer in doubt. The Prussians were at hand. The major dismounted with his adjutant-major, and placed himself in the centre of the battalion; by his orders the seventh company left the camp, crossed the road, and came to take up their position behind us, between the banks of a by-lane.

Our men had loaded their muskets, and lay concealed in the hollow of the ground. I sat down against a bush, and began to break a crust of bread, meditating on what was probably before us.

It was a fine day, and very still. We could distinctly hear the sound of a distant cannonade, two leagues off at least, towards Nogent. It was the battle of La Fourche, of which so much has been said, that had begun.

Whilst we were all in suspense, a peasant made his appearance out of the wood, and came up to speak to the major. He announced that a body of German horsemen were in occupation of a farm a few hundred yards within the coppice, reposing in perfect security; and that with twenty-five men they could be surprised and captured almost without striking a blow.

The major resolved to send a whole company, and gave orders to the first. Christian de Failly started at once, at a quick pace, at the head of his 150 men; and Captain Henri Josset, with the sixth, held himself in readiness to support him. A few moments afterwards a cannon-shot boomed right in front of us, and for the first time in my life I heard the roaring sound of the ball, as it rent the air a few yards off from where I stood.

For a quarter of an hour there was a rapid succession of discharges, and yet there was no enemy to be seen. Shells and balls came one after

[1] This declaration of certitude is reminiscent of another occasion. At Vionville on 16 August, General Bataille, a divisional commander, was breakfasting when one of his officers reported that while on patrol during the night he had seen a considerable body of enemy near at hand. The debonair General's reply was to accuse him of seeing Prussians everywhere. 'Be certain that their army is still a long way from here; and they have no, I repeat, no intention of attacking us today.' The first shells of the battle struck his camp thirty minutes later.

the other; the shells being distinguished by their distant whistling sound, which gradually grows louder and louder, till it ends in a clap of thunder as they strike the ground. I looked round; no one showed any sign of fear; a feeling of awful curiosity held us all silent. Our one desire was to know what lay hidden within the thickets on the Combres road.

We imagined it must be Christian de Failly's men who would be those to fire the first shot, for the special duty entrusted to him must have led him farther on; we therefore lent an attentive ear to every sound that came from the woods on the right. In spite of our expectations, we were taken by surprise by the violence of the platoon fire which suddenly burst forth in that direction. It went on for some minutes with the greatest vivacity, although we still could see nothing. At last the bushes 200 paces before us began to stir, and I saw two men emerging, in long capotes and glittering helmets. I had hardly descried them before they were fired at by some of our men, and at the same moment the first Prussian bullets came whistling about our ears. I could only do like the rest. I levelled my gun and disposed of several cartridges.

The fight was now along the whole line, and our desultory fire must certainly have destroyed a large number of the enemy, for the distance was short, and they were in a most exposed situation. But the breaks we made in their ranks were rapidly filled up, and the smoke now and then clearing away showed us denser and still denser masses overflowing the road and the fields, and threatening to overpower us.

My captain's orders were to fall back after having opened fire, but he determined not to retire till he was assured that it would be an absolute impossibility for us to keep the position we were holding.

We wound our way, under the shelter of the slopes of the ravine, till we reached the same height as that of the rest of the battalion; then we retraced our steps along the main road to rejoin our major. The Germans immediately advanced rapidly from the side we had just left. There was at this point only the Teilleul company, under the command of Captain de Rougé, to save us from being outflanked.

To the right, the fifth, sixth, and second companies were posted as sharpshooters in the hollow roads, and behind the bushes. Every man did his best, taking aim and firing without attending to his neighbour. Those belonging to the first were unable to fire, being placed behind the others. The major quietly gave his orders.

When the third reached the line, we began to form some idea of the immense force that was opposed to us. Colonel de M., with the battalions of the Orne, the Lower Loire, and Calvados, beat a retreat along the road to Beaumont-les-Autels; we were about 1,000 men against numbers six times greater. Our major receiving no orders, nor any aid, from Colonel de M., thought the time was come to descend to Thiron in order to reascend the opposite side, so that we might be placed under cover of the woods, he sent orders to the companies on the right to retreat by degrees. Captain de Rougé, who was sustaining the whole effort of the German right, was to remain at his post. Very soon the enemy's artillery came to take up their position on the road. One of their guns was placed in battery, not far from the path occupied by the skirmishers of Le Teilleul, who, under their brave captain, succeeded in making several murderous discharges.

Captain de Failly returned just as the retreat was beginning, with Sub-Lieutenants Josset and Sequard, and with what remained of his company. They were steaming with heat, and covered with dust. The peasant who had undertaken to guide them to the farm where they were to surprise the Prussian troops had led them, either from stupidity or treachery, into a regular ambuscade, where they found themselves suddenly exposed to a sharp platoon fire, almost from the muzzle.

Nevertheless the Barenton men had stood their ground, and instantly returned the fire; the officers had fought like common soldiers. Nowhere had the struggle, up to that moment, been so severe; it could not have lasted longer without Failly and his men being entirely destroyed.

After crossing the Nogent road we had—in order to gain our place of shelter on the plain—to climb a steep hill exposed to the enemy's fire. As soon as they perceived us coming out of the ravine they covered us with their projectiles. Several shells passed over our heads; one came and burst against a large tree with a terrific crash. Sub-Lieutenant Lesénéchal, who was close by, was riddled with splinters; he was carried off pierced by eleven wounds.

Colonel de M.'s artillery, consisting of one *mitrailleuse* and two small guns, had not yet moved from the other side of the hill; it protected our retreat by three or four discharges, and then at a rapid trot went to rejoin the main column.

On reaching the top of the hill we found ourselves on the high road leading to Beaumont-les-Autels and Authon-du-Perche, and we saw that all the troops were withdrawing in that direction. We drew up in our turn to form column; the companies had reassembled after sustaining more or less serious losses. The first alone had forty-three absent; but the whole seventh, officers included, were missing; the order to retreat sent to Captain de Rougé had been unattended to. Many were of opinion that he must have been cut off, with the best part of his men. I could learn nothing further, for my company was beginning to move, and I had to follow. As I marched on I was a prey to the most cruel anxiety. I made inquiries of all those who came up from the rear, to rejoin their ranks farther on, and at the end of half an hour a Garde Mobile told me he had seen my friend. The order to retreat never having reached him, he felt it was his duty to remain at his post; after having again and again brought back his little troop to the fire, he at last had realised that he and his men were left absolutely alone in the valley, and he then decided on rejoining the battalion. When he reached the footbridges the Germans came down from all sides into the ravine, and distinguishing him by his tall figure, made him their target; but their bullets whistled over his head, and he returned to us safe and sound. Great admiration is felt at the brave defence he has made with his 150 men against a perfect deluge of Prussians. If all our captains shared his sense of duty, France would not be where she now is.

Fernand de Rougé's account of this action is given in the following letter to his mother.

From Fernand de Rougé to La Comtesse de Rougé, Le Mans,

23 November 1870

Dear Mother,

How anxious you must be! But set your mind at rest, for I am in perfect health and safety.

At last we have seen the Prussians. On Monday morning we left Montigny, knowing that we were in danger of being overwhelmed by superior numbers. There was no time to be lost; yet, instead of being made to hasten forward, we were most imprudently drawn up at Thiron, and posted in a disadvantageous position half-way up the hill. As we were fixing our camp, we saw a party of ten Uhlans galloping full speed at no very great distance. Shortly afterwards a passer-by warned us that the enemy was approaching, and that we were on the point of being attacked. We all made our preparations. I posted my company in skirmishing order behind a ditch, and there we waited without stirring. A moment afterwards the first volley of musketry was heard. It came from 500 Prussians, who, after having drawn the first company into a snare, through the treachery of a peasant, were opening fire on our poor friend Christian. He withstood their attack with admirable coolness, and successfully repulsed them. At the first sound of the firing, my men began to take to their heels. You can imagine my fury! but I stormed at them with such effect, that they all came back to their first positions. At the end of a quarter of an hour I also began to fire, and bullets were soon flying on every side. This went on for an hour and a half, after which, the enemy continually increasing in number, our major sounded the retreat. We had before us forces ten times superior to our own, and eight pieces of cannon. I did not hear the signal for retreat; therefore, when I saw my company beginning to withdraw under the command of the lieutenant, I fell into a great rage, and by dint of shouting succeeded in getting about fifty of the men back behind the ditch. For twenty minutes I stood thus alone, exposed to the fire of the enemy. But I have nothing to boast of, for I must say that I thought we were supported by the whole battalion, and I had also no idea that the enemy's forces were so numerous. Happily, my sergeant, Nourdon, saw how the case stood, and gave me warning; but it was now very late, and the whole body of Prussians were upon us. I gave a whistle, and all my men, without thinking of flight, calmly grouped themselves round me. I made them take the direction of a sheltered road; and that I did not fall the next instant is due to a special protection from above, for the chances were a hundred to one that I should not live to get back. I had crossed the ditch last of all, when, turning round, I saw three Prussians in the act of jumping over it. I levelled my gun at them, but, to my dismay, it missed fire! A moment afterwards three bullets whizzed past my ears. I started off like the wind to rejoin my men, and we regained the battalion without loss of life, though under a perfect hailstorm of grapeshot.

I have three men wounded; Christian has six killed and about fifteen wounded. Our major and the four friends, M., Doynel, Christian, and myself, are untouched. The Prussians fire very badly; not one of us ought to have escaped. I am enchanted with my men, they showed such coolness, and gathered round me with such touching confidence. Séquard, Juhère, and Moisseron behaved splendidly.

The losses on the enemy's side, they say, are serious. A peasant who has been over the battlefield reports 500 or 600, but that, I think, must be a great exaggeration. What is certain is, that in one single corner of the field in front of my company there lay sixteen dead bodies—our men being wise enough only to fire when they could take direct aim. The most suffering time for us was the retreat. The Prussians pursued us for nearly twenty leagues, as far as Mamers.

Le Mans, 24 November 1870

We were very much fatigued, for we had been on the march since the morning without having tasted any food; but there was no time to lose. We went on at the quickest pace, passing through Beaumont-les-Autels without a moment's pause, and we marched southwards till nightfall; we were, it was said, to sleep at Authon. The men gathered up what energy they had left to reach their promised quarters; at seven we came in sight of the lights of the town. But here a cruel disappointment awaited us. Authon was inundated with soldiers from every corps; there was not a morsel of bread left, nor a glass of water, nor a corner on the straw. We had to pile arms in a marshy meadow, and after having posted sentries, the troops were dismissed with orders to fall in again in the morning at nine o'clock. A few were fortunate enough to find in the inns some scanty remnants that they could devour. At the time appointed we were again in our places, not knowing how we should be able to drag ourselves any farther if, as report said, the Prussians were pursuing us.

I drew near a group of officers who were talking very eagerly.

'It appears,' said one of them, 'that we are to march to Nogent.'

There was a general outcry. 'Are they mad!. . . March to Nogent! which is only three leagues from Thiron, when we have just gone five in the opposite direction? . . . March to Nogent! when we are told that 1,500 Prussians are already at Luigny; when we are sure to meet them, and when there is no chance of our being in fighting condition. . . . It is madness!'

The officer who had been the first to speak agreed that nothing could be more insane; but Colonel de M. had received very peremptory orders, and was determined to carry them out to the letter.

'Well,' said a captain in the battalion of Mortain, 'let us find our major, and hear what he has to say.'

They disappeared in the darkness; I then saw all the captains of the companies go past; they were going to the place where the roads of Nogent and Beaumont-les-Autels meet, to have an interview with Colonel de M. I caught a few passing words; they were speaking of holding a council of war—of taking responsibility upon themselves.

All the battalions were assembled on the road, and were jammed together in a narrow space, where they could neither move forwards nor backwards; carts were attempting to force their way through and sticking fast in the deep ruts; the crush and confusion were frightful. With all their devotion and their sense of discipline the men at last grew impatient, and asked how long they were going to be kept there, with their knapsacks on their backs and their feet in the mud. I should have been glad, indeed, if I could have told them. The night was pitch dark. I took up my position by the side of a cart, supporting my head against the shafts. I was dropping from want of sleep, and felt incapable of putting two ideas together.

At the end of two mortal hours the column seemed to be on the move; there was no longer any doubt about it, we were going to Nogent, and it was the battalion of Mortain that was appointed to take the lead and to draw on the rest of the column. The efforts of our major and of the officers had been in vain. Colonel de M. had received strict orders, and he was resolved to adhere to them, though it should cost him his life and the loss of the corps he commanded. Though very ill and in acute suffering, he mounted his horse and rode resolutely at the head of the column towards the gulf from which not one of us expected to return alive.

When we had gone two leagues we stopped for five minutes, and a great number who had not been able to keep up rejoined the ranks. During the two hours we had lost on the way it had been impossible to prevent those who were utterly worn out from sitting down in some corner and falling fast asleep; but after this first halt not another moment's rest was given; alarming reports arrived in quick succession, and we hurried on, that we might reach Nogent before the Prussians could be upon us. It was thus that, the first mistake having been committed, all the subsequent errors became inevitable; we were driven to believe that this frantic march, made without looking behind us and without drawing breath, was, in the circumstances, a necessity.

But exhaustion was beginning by degrees to overpower us. The column, encumbered with baggage-wagons, was lengthening itself out farther and farther; the men sank down upon the heaps of stones by the wayside insensible and motionless, and there we had to leave them. Our retreat seemed likely to cost us twice as much as the battle, as has been constantly the case since the war began.

When a misfortune is inevitable one makes up one's mind to it; but there is no consolation when one knows that with a little fore-thought things would have turned out differently.

I marched with half-shut eyes, stumbling against my companions and against the vehicles and horses on the road. There was no moon. From time to time bright lights, appearing on the skirts of the wood, flashed for a moment through the darkness, then all was gloom again; my captain said they were no doubt the enemy's signals. It was evident the Germans were close upon us. Every dull sound we heard might be a cannon-shot, every path through the thicket might give passage to a Uhlan. We were not in fear; but we felt that in the condition our men were in they could not possibly defend themselves, and we were reduced to put all our hope in the darkness that surrounded us.

Half-way between Authon and Nogent Colonel de M., vanquished by suffering, had to dismount; he was placed in a wagon *pêle-mêle* with all the disabled Mobiles, and resigned his command to M. de Grainville. Our major galloped on to Nogent, followed by an adju-tant, to reconnoitre the way, leaving orders for the march to be continued.

A moment's reflection had been sufficient to take away all hopes of rest—there could be no question of quarters so long as the enemy was on our flank. At Nogent we halted in the street; we sank down upon the doorsteps, and for a few minutes sat with our heads buried in our hands. Then what we had foreseen came to pass; a mounted adjutant rode up to say that we must make all haste to take the road to Bellesme, as the Prussians were on the point of entering the town. The counter-order, which we were so astonished not to have received at Authon, had, it appears, been entrusted to a countryman, who had first thought proper to take his own time, and had ended by giving up the dispatch to a gendarme. Major Grainville received it just as we were in the act, of arriving. Thus, after having made fourteen leagues[1] since morning with our knapsacks at our backs and our muskets over our shoulders, we now had on pain of death to go six more. Again we set forth. The

[1] Over thirty miles.

town was deserted; everything seemed dead. At the corner of the street I saw the major. He pointed out to me a wagon laden with ration bread, which he had discovered at the Mairie. I ran towards it with my men, and each one took what he could. Then those who were still able to march hastened to turn to the left, and to ascend the hill. Whilst we were dragging ourselves along upon this road to Bellesme the day began to dawn, and the 21 November 1870 became yesterday.

(22 November)

As far as the eye could reach the road was covered with scattered, routed soldiers; they were toiling painfully along, a few steps at a time, and then sitting down by the wayside to recover their energy. Almost all of them had got rid of their knapsacks. Now and then a cart rolled by laden with baggage and with the sick; an enormous diligence swept past like a hurricane, carrying clusters of men who were hanging on to it wherever they could lay hold. By the side of the road there were a few farmhouses, where the lucky ones of that day found a piece of black bread and a cup of milk.

The road made immense circuits, winding half-way up the hill and overlooking lovely valleys, in which the morning mists were floating. Another beautiful autumn day was beginning; the calm beauty of the landscape formed a strong contrast to the scene of desolation that was beneath our eyes.

Towards midday all these waves of men surging onwards in the same direction were massed together in the main street of Bellesme. I climbed up the steep ascent, on the top of which is perched this eagle's nest, so celebrated in the Middle Ages, and which still contains at this day a population of 3,000 souls. I went into two inns; every hole and corner had been taken by assault. At last I found anchorage in the back shop of a linendraper, where for two hours I was able to sit by the fireside. Many soldiers had taken shelter, as I had done, in this hospitable dwelling; two kind ladies gave us food and drink, and gazed at us with their large eyes filled with compassion.

At every step we had taken, the disaster appeared to me to become greater; it was not only the corps of Colonel de M., it was a part of Fierrec's army, perhaps the whole of that army, which was now suddenly retreating twenty leagues. At Bellesme there were soldiers of all sorts coming from every part of Perche and Beauce; all that fertile country which we had occupied two days before was now in the power of the Grand Duke of Mecklenburg.

Colonel de M. having obtained a few days' leave of absence, our major was placed provisionally, by order of the colonel, and also by right of seniority, at the head of all the battalions which had come from Illiers, and Captain Montécot, an old officer of the line, took the command of the battalion of Mortain.

There was an idea of resting forty-eight hours at Bellesme, and we were beginning to breathe a little, when Captain Montécot received order to go and occupy the post of Saint-Jean-la-Forêt, three kilo-metres behind the town,[1] and to spend the night there. About 600 men had to be laboriously gathered together again, and we took a by-road which was to lead us to our destination. This road descended into a narrow ravine, and terminated in a cul-de-sac; it was like the valley of Thiron, on a smaller scale.

When we heard that the Prussians were not far off, we thought it would have been difficult to select a better spot than this for the extermination of the battalion of Mortain. . . . As we advanced the signs of danger increased. The enemy's cavalry showed themselves here and there on the crest of the hills, and we could hear the report of musketry. Our column was more than 500 paces in length; for the greater part of the men could not keep up, and rather dragged themselves along than marched. My captain sent me on several times in front, mounted on Bismarck (a hideous horse taken from King William's Uhlans), to endeavour to persuade Captain Montécot to turn back, since it was evident that the post we were being sent to was not tenable, and that we should be destroyed to the last man, without having the power of defending ourselves. I was unable to convince the old soldier. As he could not succeed in meeting death at Thiron, by exposing himself recklessly to the enemy's fire that he might set an example to his men, I conclude he wished to terminate his long career in this defile. I quite understood under our present circum-stances the desire he felt to court death, even for no purpose; but I cannot say I shared it. 'I have strict orders,' he said to me, 'and it is my duty to obey them.' At that instant the firing burst forth upon our left in a long, dismal rolling sound. I looked at the captain. 'Give orders to fall back, sir,' were his only words. I did not stay to hear them repeated, but regained the end of the column at a sharp trot.

On returning to Bellesme, we learnt that a gendarme had been sent

[1] To the east of the town.

to recall us; no doubt he had lost his way. The firing we had heard on our left was from the Pontifical Zouaves, who had come no one knows from whence, and were defending the approaches to the town against the German vanguard, so as to give time to General Rousseau's troops to retreat to Mamers. Thus Captain Viallet had indubitably, by his wisdom and firmness, preserved the battalion of Mortain from total destruction.

I was confounded on seeing that after having gone twenty leagues we were still closely pressed. When should we be in safety? No doubt we shall have to start again this evening, and resume this hopeless and apparently interminable retreat. The Germans must have made a large number of prisoners. . . . Would it not have been better to have allowed ourselves to be overwhelmed at Thiron or at Authon, and to have sold our lives, than to be hunted and run down like deer? . . . Who knows? . . . Can—ought the soldier to understand anything which lies out of the immediate circle of his company? Let us march, and follow, as our superior officers order, till we drop; and, above all, let us think as little as we can.

Whilst the men, having fallen out for five minutes, were besieging the doors of the inns and the bakers' shops, I tried to pick up a little news. Our baggage was saved; but two horses belonging to our major and to his adjutant had been lost at Thiron. Rest, sleep, are out of the question. Admiral Jaurès has just arrived, and given his orders. We are to start again immediately; this time for Mamers, four leagues off. We set out in pretty good order, from sixty to eighty men in each company, keeping very tolerably in line. But soon they all begin again to falter, till at last each one goes his own way, and gets over the ground as he can. The same suspicious lights we saw between Authon and Nogent again from time to time cast a flickering glimmer across our line of march. All do their best not to be left behind; they hang on to the wagons and the gun-carriages. At eleven o'clock we enter Mamers. The townspeople hasten to open their houses to us. Beauce is already far behind, and we find ourselves again in the hospitable west. I entered the first door I saw open. I snatched a morsel of food, and sank down upon a bed.

I had for a few hours been enjoying the heavenly blessing of forgetfulness, when I was awoke by the drums beating with a great noise in the street. We were setting out again. There was no longer any possibility of a regular transmission of orders; but some of the officers went up and down the street, giving notice in a low voice to the sergeants and corporals; that we were going to take the road to La Hutte.

It was five o'clock; about forty men belonging to the third company succeeded in reappearing, and we did what we never thought we could have done—we marched.

(23 November)

Daylight, when it came, revealed a sky laden with clouds; and, to add to our miseries, the rain began to fall in torrents. Till then the weather had, at least, been mild and dry. Soon our clothes were saturated; the road was transformed into a river; thousands of men, shivering and soaked to the skin, were floundering in the ruts. All who could find a place in a carriage or on a gun had perched themselves up on it any way they could. We were flying in every sort of way, and in every description of vehicle—tilted carts, broughams, basket-carriages, *chars-à-bancs.* No one who had any sense of the ludicrous could have refrained from thinking of the *Embarras de Paris*; but we were in no humour for laughing.

All this was passing yesterday, and already I am turning it into a page of history, ardently hoping that I may not have many more such pages to record. At twelve o'clock we reached La Hutte, after having made from six to seven leagues. We were told: 'Two more, and you will have got to the end. At Beaumont-sur-Sarthe[1] you will take the railroad.' And we have made these two leagues more. Counting the thirty-four we have gone since we left Montigny, you will know how far a Norman soldier can march, without having had more than two meals in all, and five hours' sleep. At Beaumont-sur-Sarthe, M. de Petitville, major of the fourth battalion of Calvados, had begun to fill the railway-carriages which were destined for us with his own men. Happily, our major was there, and had them restored to us. On arriving at Le Mans, the men were so cramped and stiffened with sitting in the carriages that there were not more than two or three of them who could stand upright. In this state they had to drag themselves on to the Place des Jacobins, half a league from the station. There they piled arms. It was midnight, and they were turned into the cathedral, where they passed the rest of the night, without straw and without coverings.

[1] Half-way along the road from Alençon to Le Mans.

Just now I went to look at them. A few bundles of straw had been found for the disabled. There was a great crowd—some sitting, some lying at full length, their clothes in rags, their eyes sunken, their faces black with dust. The ladies of Le Mans were passing to and fro amongst them, dispensing food, clothing, and kind words, and approaching, without disgust, all the miserable objects who had found shelter within those walls.

That scene, lit up by a ray of sunshine that came streaming through the painted windows and fell across the pavement, was worthy of being painted; I shall never forget it.

At this morning's roll-call, about 200 men were missing. I believe we did not lose more than sixty at the battle of Thiron. When we were marching to Nogent I thought that the journal of this battalion had come to its last page. . . . No doubt—thanks to the darkness—the Germans never saw us; perhaps they, too, were worn out. At any rate, we had a great escape.

I have read this long, sad story over again, after an interval of four months. I will not take away one word from it, however prolix and monotonous it may appear. Now that the war is over, Thiron will remain our most important battle; melancholy as have been all the other battles of this war, excepting Rezonville, Coulmiers, Villepain-en-Beauce, and Bapaume; but honourable for the soldiers of Mortain, and glorious for our major and for two of my friends, if glory is the reward of devotion, and not only of success. For our generals may say what they like; the ground once abandoned, the victory is lost, even if an attack is successfully repulsed, or a retreat successfully accomplished. We may, however, say, as did Villars after Malplaquet, that many such defeats as these might possibly have saved France, since the enemy sustained much heavier losses than we did. Every one knows it is not the fire of the Germans that has destroyed the Garde Mobile, but the tactics of our generals. . . .

I am far from saying that a different line of conduct on the part of our leaders during those two days could have had any important influence on the ultimate fate of the war, but it is mistakes of detail, which, when multiplied, bring disastrous consequences. And successes in smaller things would have completely changed the aspect of affairs in Le Perche, Le Dunois, and the Chartrain country, if a sensible direction had been given to this campaign of October and November. Why were all those battalions echelonned from Verneuil to Châteaudun? We have learnt since that they were intended to prevent the Mecklenburg army from advancing and overpowering our army of the Loire by joining hands with Prince Frederick Charles, who was coming from Metz.

They would have accomplished this object if each major had employed one half of his men in harassing the Germans and cutting off their supplies, and the other half in rendering the defiles of Perche and Normandy inaccessible. . . . What the Vendeans did in their day with scythes and pitchforks, the Normans could have achieved, I imagine, with their *chassepot* rifles. But, in order to obtain these results, the commanders of the various corps should have enjoyed more freedom of action; the struggle should have been allowed to preserve its character as a national contest; and a mere declaiming barrister, intoxicated by the sound of his presumptuous verbiage, should not have played at soldiers on a large scale with Count von Moltke and Prince Frederick Charles. Then, who knows what might have happened? Would these infallible tacticians have accomplished by their talents what the blunders of Gambetta and his party saved them the trouble of? It is possible; but it is difficult to admit the absolute infallibility of people who have just outdone the greatest errors of Napoleon I, by taking Alsace and part of Lorraine. R.M.

IV

The Army of the Loire

On 22 November the German General Headquarters at Versailles decided that there were now no further dangers from the Army of the West, and ordered the Grand Duke of Mecklenburg to turn his attention to the Army of the Loire. The Detachment which, after the capture of Nogent-le-Rotron, was heading towards Le Mans was to assist Prince Frederick Charles by attacking the French either in the flank at Orleans or across their lines of communication to seize the bridge at Beaugency or Blois. By 24 November the Grand Duke was so situated that his forces could reach any of these objectives within forty-eight hours. It was with the establishment of this cooperation between the Detachment and the Second Army that the French chance of a successful break through to Paris came virtually to an end. The small flame of success which had been lit in the darkness of the French defeats by the victory of Coulmiers was dying down and was soon to be finally extinguished.

Like the Prussians, the French realised that if the Army of the Loire collapsed it would endanger their whole position in the Loire valley below Orleans. They therefore decided to divert attention from this flank, and at the same time further their purpose of an advance towards Paris, by switching their effort to the other side. A successful attack on the left flank of the Prussian Army opposite Gien would open the way to Fontainebleau and possibly thereafter to the capital. In consequence, on 28 November the right wing of the Army of the Loire, after occupying Montargis, launched an attack at Baune la Rolande. Although the attack was unsuccessful, the manoeuvre alarmed the Prussians, who began to echelon their troops towards the East to meet this new threat. On 29 November, the Grand Duke of Mecklenburg's Detachment, which for so long had been hounding the Army of the West, rejoined the Second Army and reverted to the command of Prince Frederick Charles, north-west of Orleans.

So far no news had arrived from Paris. Then, on 30 November, a dispatch arrived. It had been sent by balloon, but caught by contrary winds had landed in Norway. Now four days late it arrived at Tours. The news it contained was dramatic: 'On Tuesday 29 November, the Army of the Exterior, commanded by General Ducrot, our most energetic commander, will attack the enemy fortified positions and will, if he takes them, push on towards the Loire, probably in the direction of Gien.' If the sortie had gone as planned, it was already under way, and 100,000 troops from Paris were about to break out into the open country to the south to meet the Army of Loire, probably in the Forest of Fontainebleau. Cost what it might, the Army of the Loire must go forward to meet them with food, ammunition and victory.

But the sortie had not gone as planned. On the night of the 28th the Marne south of Paris flooded its banks and the assault had to be postponed for twenty-four hours. When Ducrot's men did cross, on the 30th, surprise had been lost and they were unable to reach the plateau beyond the city. The only real success had been a diversionary attack carried out by the Marines on the opposite side of the city, where they had occupied the small village of Epinay, near St Denis. Notwithstanding, an exultant signal was sent off by balloon. Mentioned in this dispatch was the capture of Epinay. This name, coupled with the glowing account of the sortie given by the balloonists, led the Delegation at Tours to believe that the village involved was Epinay-sur-Orge, a village situated some twelve miles south of Paris and well behind the Prussian lines. The inference was that Ducrot had broken the ring and was well on the way towards Fontainebleau. It was enough to set the whole Army of the Loire in motion. The two Corps on the right would attack again at Beaune la Rolande, while 15 and 16 Corps under General Chanzy would advance astride the Orleans-Paris road. 17 Corps would remain to guard Orleans, supported as necessary by 21 Corps, which was arriving at Vendôme under the command of Admiral Jaurès. This was the Corps to which belonged the Battalion of Mortain.

Advancing on the left on 1 December, Chanzy achieved some initial success, reaching almost to the village of Loigny. But when he resumed his efforts on the 2nd, the enemy had been reinforced and by the evening his forces were spent. At the same time Prince Frederick Charles had received a peremptory order from General Headquarters. Von Moltke's attention had been for some time turned towards Ducrot. Now that the sortie had been defeated he could resume the control which he had previously exercised in the south. Reassume it he did, with a decisiveness which paid little attention to anything that had happened in the last few days. 'Tomorrow,' he ordered, '3 December, the Second Prussian Army and the Detachment will advance in a concentric attack against Orleans.'

On 3 December the German forces advanced methodically. Each French strongpoint was subjected to intense artillery preparation before the infantry were launched against it. It soon became apparent to d'Aurelle de Paladines that a general retreat was the only thing that could save the army. Abandoning hope of saving Orleans, he ordered his various corps to fall back from where they stood. As a result, the army was divided, with the Loire between the two halves. It was left to Gambetta, having removed d'Aurelle from his command, to impose some logic on this result by renaming that part to the east of the river as the First Army of the Loire, under General Bourbaki, and that to the west as the Second. This Second Army of the Loire consisted of 16, 17 and 21 Corps (by now at Marchénoir) and was placed under the command of General Chanzy. For a moment, Gambetta contemplated a return to the attack with the First Army, but was quick to realise this was impossible. The troops were in complete confusion and pouring back unchecked. On 10 December the Delegation was forced to withdraw the seat of government from Tours to Bordeaux.

Yet while this rout was taking place to the east of the Loire, something very different was happening to the West. The Second Army had found itself a commander. Chanzy was younger (he was forty-seven) and plainly abler than the majority of his compatriots of equal rank. The greater part of his service had been in Algiers, whence he had arrived too late to be tainted with those feelings of hopelessness that afflicted most of the commanders who had been involved in the earlier parts of the campaign under Napoleon III. He saw that to continue the retreat in the state of morale induced by the repeated defeats since Loigny would expose his young troops to the danger of a complete debacle. Although it may not have been apparent to Roger de Mauni, the withdrawal along the west bank of the Loire was a planned and generally well conducted operation. Until 10 December Chanzy stood and defended himself between the Forest of Marchenoir and the river. Only when the enemy reached Blois and threatened to cross the river in his rear did he abandon the Loire valley and seek the protection of the river Loir about Vendôme. (The similarity between the names of the two rivers is confusing.) Here again he remained for as long as he dared and only on the 16th, when the danger of being out-flanked from the south again became too great, did he continue the retreat. By now in spite of his devoted leadership the situation of his troops was desperate and it is doubtful if they could have resisted further. They were saved by two fortuitous events. The first was a rumour that reached Prince Frederick Charles that Gien was being attacked. Though later proved false, this was sufficient for him at the time to seek authority to call off pursuit beyond Vendôme. The second was a revised concept of operation issued by von Moltke on 17 December, that 'the pursuit of the enemy after defeat should be carried no farther than is necessary to disperse his force or the main part of it, so that it shall be rendered incapable of rallying again for some time.' The intention was to avoid the exhaustion of constantly following up small bands, to wait until the enemy forces grew into organised armies and to deal with them by short and rapid attacks. In consequence, the final part of Chanzy's retreat was hampered more by the weather than by the enemy so that he was able to gain the protection of the Sarthe at Le Mans on 19 December.

The Army of the Loire had always been the focal point of French activity in the provinces. Nevertheless, there were other areas of French resistance which had formed, as it were, two wings stretching out north and east from the seat of government at Tours. The left wing ran from Le Mans, through Rouen, Amiens and Arras to the fortress area of Lille on the Belgian border. The right ran along the Loire, across the valley of the Saône and via the fort-resses of Besançon, Belfort and Langres to the Vosges. The left wing was badly dented, with Rouen captured on 15 December; the centre was gone with the dispersion of the Army of the Loire and the withdrawal of the government to Bordeaux. It was to the right wing that Gambetta now turned for salvation. For this purpose the First Loire Army, under the command of General Bourbaki, was to be moved by train to the Saône valley to join up with other forces fighting in the area, including those of the ageing revolu-tionary Garibaldi, with orders to relieve the siege of Belfort and to cut the German lines of communication with Paris. It will be heard later how they fared.

Meanwhile, although the main emphasis was shifting to the east the left wing was still capable of some activity, particularly as it held the two most able generals in the French command; Chanzy at Le Mans, and the legendary Faidherbe in command of the Army of the North. Yet what little freedom of action remained to them was always threatened by the possibility of the Prussian forces being reinforced. Even so, by 28 December Chanzy was sending out two Mobile columns to clear the country of enemy in the direction of Vendôme and another to reconnoitre towards Nogent. When they met with some success, Chanzy was encouraged to submit his further plans to the government at Bordeaux. These plans were for a simultaneous approach on Paris by himself from the west, by Faidherbe from the north and by Bourbaki from the east. Since these plans did not accord with the greater design that Gambetta had for Bourbaki, Chanzy was advised to wait until the middle of January, by which time there would be two new corps to help him. In the meantime he could make his preliminary dispositions.

This is an appropriate place to pause to look back to see what Roger de Mauni made of the events of these past five weeks. When the Mortain battalion set out from Le Mans on 27 November, they had thought they were headed for Paris.

Sargé, Saturday, 26 November

We had one day only in which to rest ourselves. Yesterday morning we again had to make ready, and go on to Sargé, a village one league's distance from Le Mans. I can scarcely believe the Prussians can be close at hand. But we take every precaution as if we expected an attack from one moment to another; a company of the line now marching with us has had to furnish fifty sentries, and ourselves sixty. The rain, always so ready to favour us, has not failed us today.

If this hard life lasts much longer there will be very few of us left. Captain de Failly is already very ill, and with all his energy he will not be able to go much farther. Captains Montécot and De Quigny, and Lieutenant Queslier, are quite incapacitated, and have been obliged to ask for leave of absence. Many of the men are absolutely incapable of marching another step.

Le Mans, Sunday, 27 November, morning

It would seem as if the one great object was to wear us out. Yesterday I obtained leave to go into the town to breakfast. When I returned to the camp I heard that we were to take up our position half a league off, at a small deserted château. whose name I have forgotten. This change of quarters occupied the whole afternoon. At 9 p.m. we had pitched our tents, made our soup, and put out all our fires, when a fresh order arrived; we were immediately to strike the camp and return to Le Mans, which we accordingly did without an instant's delay. On our return, which took place at midnight, we received the derisive order to encamp under the trees of the public promenade, by the theatre, upon the wet and dirty ground. The men dispersed; those who had any spirit left went and knocked at the doors of the houses, begging for shelter; many sank down, overcome with weariness, on the banks of the Allée, and there remained till daylight.

This morning the roll was called at nine. Our only idea today is of marching to the front. We are on the way to Paris: we shall be there in a month, in a fortnight. . . . Can it be possible that our generals have suddenly taken an energetic step? . . . I fear, on the contrary, that we are every day losing our head more and more, and that we are becoming the mere sport of chance! . . . A quarter to nine; it is time to close this note-book, and to go where destiny leads us. . . .

Camp de Grand-Lucé, Tuesday, 29 November

I have re-read what I wrote last Sunday. It is full of sadness and discouragement; but If I had known what we have had to go through during these last two days, I doubt if I should have had the heart to write at all. Never mind; so long as I have a bit of pencil or scrap of paper left, I shall go on with these notes—destined though they doubt-less are to perish with their author; for we must not conceal the fact from ourselves, that what we suffered in the retreat of Nogent is nothing compared to what now lies before us. . . .

Here we are on the march again, in the direction of Tours. . . . Can it be that we are going to the rescue of France? We should be very presumptuous if we dared to hope that she might rise victorious; . . . but we have the consolation of knowing that we are almost certain not to survive her defeat. If only we might die gloriously, as some of our friends have done! But I have a presentiment that we shall, many of us, fall victims to the cold, the privations, the miseries of every kind which must be our inevitable portion. Till today the weather has been mild; but that cannot last—what shall we do, what will our unhappy men do, without greatcoats and without trousers, when the hard frosts set in? Many in my company have not even a rug for their night covering.

It was the day before yesterday—the roll had just been called on the public promenade, where we had been dismissed on our return from Sargé, when we heard that the Gardes Mobiles were just going to receive their field rations, and that afterwards they were to go to the cartridge stores, and rejoin the army that same day. Scarcely had we received our instructions, when the field rations arrived. Each company was to get its portion of bread, bacon, sugar, coffee, salt, and rice. Up to that day the men of the 30th Regiment had catered for themselves, at their own expense, receiving twenty sous a day; but from this time they are to receive twenty-five sous and their food besides. This alteration has become a necessity, for we now form part of a large army, passing through a country that has been laid waste and desolate. The trees by the roadside have been stripped of their apples, and the peasants hide away their last remaining stores in the depths of their cellars. But if all the issues of food are made like that on Sunday, many of the men will be driven either to go marauding or else to die of hunger. The rations were given out at random; some corps got too much, whilst others received next to nothing. However, the men got off, on this first occasion, better than might have been expected. Each one made what haste he could to tie his portion of bread and bacon over his knapsack; but so great was the hurry in which we were sent off to the cartridge stores, that I saw as I went large masses of meat left behind, which there had been no time to cut up. We are for ever wanting in calmness and self-possession. An order comes—on the instant we fly off, leaving everything to its fate; and we have not gone 200 paces before we are drawn up in the street, and left to stand there, shivering, under arms for an hour.

Nothing was less like a 'distribution' than the pillage which took place at eleven o'clock at the wagons containing the cartridge stores. When we got to them, no one was there; there was nothing for it but to take possession of the first barrels we could lay hold of, and give each man what he required for ninety rounds. Just as we had concluded this operation, and our major was receiving an order from the general to advance with the utmost speed upon the road to Pontlieue, the officer in charge of the park came up in a furious rage, threatening us, right and left, with 'complaints' and 'arrests'. We let him talk, and proceeded to force our way with all the haste we could through the streets blocked up with men, horses, and vehicles.

On the footpaths were numbers of troops of the line, who appeared to be waiting for our departure before starting on the same road. At two o'clock we had reached the last outskirts, and were on the road leading to Tours, through La Châtre. It was rumoured in the ranks that we were to march till night; a few moments' halt would have been of great service; but it seems the salvation of France demanded that on that day we should go without our dinners!

I strove, as I marched along, to come to some conclusion as to what was going on, but it was no easy task. When I reflected on events in general, I could see nothing but hopeless confusion; the few papers I had been able to get at Le Mans had given me very little information. When I arrived there I had believed that all was over, at all events for the present. The scene of disorganisation I had witnessed during those three days appeared to me an irretrievable catastrophe. Yet here we are setting out again, half-equipped, and quite unrecruited—and for what destination? For the south, for the Army of the Loire, they tell us, which is marching upon Paris. . . . What had we been doing these three last weeks? What were M. Gambetta's intentions? I calculated that the German Army of Metz must have reached Étampes by 15 November, and have left the corps of Mecklenburg and of Von der Tann free to advance; but how could it be supposed that not one amongst our general officers should have contemplated this possibility?

Raising my eyes I beheld, in the visible chaos which was unrolling itself along the ex-imperial high road, a reflection of the moral chaos into which I had fallen.

We were marching on the left-hand side of the road. On the right, all crowded, pressed, entangled together, were horses, cannon, artillery drags, ambulance carriages, soldiers, gendarmes. . . . All this immense throng moved onwards, everyone in a state of altercation with his neighbour, either because he was going too fast or because he was lagging behind—this was the army on its march. 'Forty thousand men are in front of us,' said someone, by way of encouragement. 'No, a hundred thousand,' said another, who knew just as little about it. . . . My heart was oppressed—all that I saw and heard filled me either with vexation or anxiety.

Night was falling as we entered Parigné-l'Évèque, where it was said we were to sleep. To judge by the size of the first houses we passed, it must be a large village. When we got into the centre of it, we halted; the road was choked with troops, and it was pitch dark. Though every doorway was besieged by an importunate throng, and the houses were full to overflowing, still it was cheering to see the bright candlelight in the windows. A little patience, I thought, and quarters will be assigned to us; we shall find some corner by a fireside, and a morsel of food to put between our teeth. But no: when we had stood there for half an hour, the column moved on down the street; soon the last houses disappeared, and the gleaming lights in the windows were exchanged for an immense red glare, which lit up half the sky before us—they were encamping. I could hear in the distance, round the fires, the sound of shouts, jests, oaths, disputes; and in the midst of all a plaintive melody, sung in chorus by a company of marines, was breaking in upon these discordant noises, and ascending to the skies. Wearied out as I was, I thought I had never heard anything more poetical.

After a succession of halts, necessitated by the enormous crowd, our turn arrived; we took a rough path to the right, and marched 500 steps amongst the fires and tents, and then received orders to encamp under the shelter of a fir wood, which was rapidly disappearing under the hatchets of the Mobiles. The men had fuel, and made what use they could of a few camp kettles that were still left, to make their soup; water was very scarce; as to straw, we had to do without it. I had no food, tent, or rug; someone out of charity gave me a morsel of bread, and I lay down at the foot of a tree. A few steps beyond me Christian de Failly lay rolled up in his cloak, in a hollow of the ground. The weather was particularly mild for the time of year, yet I remember suffering very much from cold.

The next morning I had to inform my company that our captain, M. Viallet, was appointed to the military commissariat, where his services were needed, and that he would be away for a long time. It was a great vexation to himself, and for us a very serious loss.

At nine o'clock the interminable column set itself again in motion, with a little less confusion than when we left Le Mans. The day before we marched fifteen kilometres and we went no greater distance today; but our halts have been so protracted and so often repeated that we reached our quarters only at nightfall, which is a serious inconvenience. We came through a very fine country, planted with large fir woods and broken by beautiful valleys. At three o'clock the five battalions of La Manche and a battalion of marine infantry were drawn up on the piece of level ground to the left of the road, and we saw riding down the line, on a large chestnut horse, a marine officer very short in stature, with a determined expression of countenance, high forehead, aquiline nose, and with black curly hair disappearing under a cap glittering with gold lace. 'That', said one of the officers, 'is General du Temple.'

I then learnt that for the present the 30th Marching Regiment had ceased to exist, and that the five battalions of La Manche were from henceforth to form part of the Army of the West, or Second Army of the Loire,[1] 21 Corps, third division, brigade Du Temple. The name of the general of the division was Guyon; the general-in-chief was a naval officer, called Jaurès; as to the generalissimo, he was unknown. Some said it was Kératry, others Jaurès, or Aurelle de Paladines; on this point I could gain no certain intelligence.

Whilst we were drawn up in brigade, a few knapsacks and rugs, which seemed to have appeared by magic, were distributed; some other articles of camp equipage were also given out. Then I heard M. de Grainville's voice in the distance giving the word of command, 'Half sections—right!' And it was in this new order of march that we arrived at Grand-Lucé.

We had pitched our tents and begun our soup, when we received orders from General du Temple to remove the camp a kilometre farther on. When we reached our new quarters we were told it was not to be there; but as in the thick darkness we were in it would have been impossible to find anything better, our major took it upon himself to let us remain. That night was passed not more agreeably than the one preceding. Today there is a distribution of rations, and we are resting. No one would imagine that in this hollow we are guarding a position; it is, nevertheless, officially announced to be the fact. The enemy is at a distance; none of the peasants we have met with have seen anything of the Prussians. They are said to be massed in the forest of Vibraye, to the north-east of Le Mans.

This morning there has been in each company a special muster, in distinction to that which we have every day. Since Thiron, each company has fallen on an average from a 1, 60 to 140 men. Many, who would have been set on their legs again by two or three days' rest, have had to be left behind at Le Mans, from their inability to go farther.

[1] This anticipates the division of the Army of the Loire, which did not in fact take place until 6 December.

Amongst the officers missing are Captains Montécot and De Quigny, Lieutenant Queslier, Sub-Lieutenant Lesénéchal, and the Surgeon-Major Bidard. . . .

Thus the number of the battalion has been reduced by nearly 300 since we left Cherbourg; the retreat to Nogent has cost us dear. There are those who maintain that it has had the effect of hardening the men. I do not believe it. Those whose physical strength has withstood the trial are possibly better soldiers than they were before; but the moral injury it has done is irreparable. This campaign in Perche has deprived the troops of all confidence in their generals, in themselves, and in the star of France. This fatal effect will long be felt; it will be very difficult, if an emergency arises, to keep the men together, and to prevent those who have no sense of duty from going each one his own way.

From the Camp of Saint-Calais, Thursday, 1 December

Yesterday morning, at nine o'clock, we left the beautiful valley of Grand-Lucé, and changing our direction suddenly we marched to Saint Calais. The Prussians made their appearance in the town a few days ago; but they came in small numbers, and did not remain.

A by-road, twenty kilometres in length, brought us to Saint-Calais, through the villages of Tresson, Evaillé, and Sainte-Cerotte, and over a hilly and picturesque country. Half-way we had an hour's halt. On reaching the town we went through it without pausing, and marched another league along the road to Le Mans. Then we encamped on a plain exposed to every wind that blows, and far from all the necessaries of life. It seems a settled point that for some time to come we are not to sleep under a roof. . . .

This morning an order from the general, expressed in the severest terms, forbids every soldier or officer to enter the town; so that we cannot even hope to get a rug or a pair of shoes. These restrictions are perhaps necessary for the maintenance of order; but in the condition we are in, destitute of the most indispensable articles, they are highly inconvenient.

Yesterday was fine; but the wind has changed, and we began to feel the cold. Today a pale sunshine is lighting up the plain, whitened by the hoar-frost. Winter set in last night, I do not know what would have become of me if I had not been able to procure a rug and the canvas of a tent.

We are no doubt to pass the night again on this icy plain; but I have given up all endeavours to understand anything of what is going on either here or elsewhere.

The cold is becoming more and more severe; all is hard and frozen; we can only get water by melting the ice. Men and beasts are suffering greatly. This morning, by the general's orders, we had to drill for two hours. . . . The Prussians are reported to be down below to the north; but we can neither see nor hear anything.

The Surgeon-Major Bidard, who disappeared at Thiron, has come back today. He was for three days prisoner in the hands of the Prussians; he spent his time in attending to the wounded, both theirs and ours, and was released in virtue of the Convention of Geneva. The Prussian corps with which we were engaged was, it appears, from 10,000 to 15,000 in number. The Germans lost in that encounter a colonel and 500 men. Engagements which, like this one, are carried on almost entirely by musketry fire, are often to the disadvantage of the enemy, from the great superiority of the *chassepot* over the needle-gun.

All these facts have given us a little heart again; whatever may happen, the men of Mortain will be able to return to their homes with heads erect.

Friday, 2 December, 10 a.m.

At last we are to leave this scene of misery and freezing, where we have been spending the whole day, with the smoke in our eyes and the wind in our ears, our feet roasting at the fire and our shoulders and backs shivering with cold. We are going to Vendôme, and may soon expect to see the Prussians. It is now an hour since we began to file off; the battalions of Guyon's division are deploying laboriously one after the other on the high road to Saint-Calais. Now the artillery is beginning to move with a tremendous rumbling over the frozen furrows; in a quarter of an hour our turn will come. Pencil and paper must be put up. Standing like this, one's feet get frozen; the men stray from the ranks to light immense bonfires of straw, and crowd round the flames. . . . I am blinded with the smoke. . . . No event of importance yesterday. Rugs, so greatly needed, have been distributed; eleven men in my company had nothing to pass the night in but their loose jackets.

Captain de Failly has left for Le Mans, worn out by fever, and at the end of his strength. He hopes to return in a few days; but I fear that he is seriously ill. It will be difficult to replace him.

The Camp, near Vendôme, Saturday, 3 December

Yesterday morning we halted for a moment a league beyond Saint-Calais, near a crossway where the roads to Mondoubleau and Château-Renault meet. There is an inn there, which bears traces of blood on its walls. Some Prussians had passed that way three days before and shot a peasant.

On the signpost was the name of 'Brou' sixty kilometres to the north. I fell to thinking of that good time when we had laughed because our major predicted that the day would come when we should regret Luigny. Now I look upon Luigny as a land of promise, and Brou appears to me a terrestrial paradise.

After marching four leagues, we encamped at the village of Epuisay; the cold was terrible.

The country between Epuisay and Vendôme, which we came through this morning, is delightful. We disturbed the silence of several deep and wooded valleys, with broad streams flowing through them, which must give in summer many cool and shady retreats. Now all is stripped and bare, and besides this, nothing casts such a gloom over the face of nature as this dark and hideous trail of war, which leaves behind it such horror and desolation.

We were ordered to halt on the top of a hill, from whence we could see the towers of Vendôme.

The men took the poles out of the vineyards and made fires with them, and sat in a circle round the burning firebrands. Part of the Army of the Loire was said to be passing through Vendôme at that moment; and at the same time came another joyful piece of news. General Ducrot was declared to have made a sortie from Paris with 100,000 men, on 29 November, and to have beaten the Prussians, and taken possession of the banks of the Marne.[1] Paris was perhaps saved. It was rumoured also that a great victory had been gained at Montargis by General d'Aurelle.[2] No doubt these good tidings were not at all

[1] As already recorded, Ducrot's unsuccessful sortie did not take place until 30 November.

[2] Montargis had been occupied on 26 November and the battle of Beaune la Rolande on the right wing of the Army of the Loire was fought on 28–29 November.

true; but evidently there was something in them. Was the fate of arms perhaps on the point of changing hands? In any case, there was some gleam of hope; and that was saying a great deal. From that moment our miseries appeared less unendurable; and when, after passing through Vendôme, we made a decided turn to the north by the highroad to Paris, I felt consoled for all I had suffered.

Not that our present situation is agreeable; the battalion is on outpost duty, and my company is in the worst position; and to heighten our enjoyments, we are forbidden to light a fire. The plain we occupy is called the plain of Bel-Air—and truly it is well aired! The north wind sweeps over a distance of two leagues across the valley to beat into our faces, and it is raining and snowing together. But all that is nothing—we are on the way to Paris;[1] tomorrow no doubt we shall have gone farther. Close by is the kilometric milestone marked 176—forty-four leagues more. . . . The day when this army makes a triumphal entry into the great rescued city would be the most glorious day of my life.

The Camp, near Morée, Sunday, 4 December

It has been a hard day; it has never been so cold yet. We have marched five leagues, going northwards the whole way; an icy wind blistered our faces and ears—unhappy those who had no hood! The officers on horseback had to dismount and walk, for fear of being frozen to their saddles. We went through the villages of Pezou, Fontaine, Fréteval, and we have encamped near the large town of Morée, amongst the vineyards, as we did yesterday. Already many acres have been robbed of their poles, and many of the vines have perished in the flames, victims of sad misunderstandings. The general had said 'Spare them!' but one must live, and I could hardly blame the man who should set the town on fire if it was to give us any warmth. . . . The night will not be a pleasant one . . . but what does it signify? We are on our way to Paris. . . . Each of the two Armies of the Loire reckons, they say, 150,000 men. France has chosen this as its rendezvous for the extermination of the German hordes. . . .

This country is full of ruins. On the hill overlooking Fréteval there is a beautiful old tower; but everywhere there are remains of ancient

---

[1] Even by this time, 3 December, the battle of Loigny had been lost and there was no hope of a further advance on Paris.

days. This is the valley of the Loir, the river slaps at our feet under a thick bed of ice, the sun has sunk in fog and rime;—behind the opposite heights there lies the forest of the Gaudinière, on the way to Mondoubleau and Le Mans. For the last two days I have been able to look in that direction without regret; after all, we never can be more miserable than we are now.

Camp of La Colombe, Tuesday, 6 December

I have had to renounce the exciting pastime of counting the kilometres on the Paris road. Yesterday morning the head of the column turned to the right, the valley of the Loir disappeared, and we found ourselves again, as if by magic, in the midst of Beauce. Fields denuded of trees, hideous villages, avaricious and selfish country people. Nothing is wanting; and with all this, no horizon. The imperceptible undulations of the ground prevent one from seeing more than two or three kilometres of the landscape; sometimes, fifty paces before us, a native suddenly starts up out of a hollow. This view of ups and downs is very monotonous. We have had three leagues of it, and now we have encamped near La Colombe, a dreary village destitute of everything.

The only wood to be had is out of the neighbouring forest,[1] which is half a league distant. Our hospitable villagers have carried off the ropes from the wells, and stare at us with disdainful looks as we make our soup with water out of the ponds, and eat our crusts of frozen bread, as hard as iron.

The number of sick is increasing, and that of the effectives constantly diminishing. General du Temple seems to fear lest we should suffer from an excess of rest; today we have had three hours' drill. It is so bitterly cold that the men can scarcely hold their muskets.

Captain Montécot is come back, after having passed two days at Saint-Hilaire-du-Harcouët; he is far from being recovered. His company has been given back to him, and M. de Gerval has been appointed captain of the third, in the place of M. Viallet.

This morning a report is in circulation which I will not believe. Orleans is said to be evacuated by us, and retaken by the Prussians; this would indeed be past all comprehension.[2] What makes me fearful,

[1] The Forest of Marchénoir.

[2] Unfortunately true. Orleans was reoccupied on 4 December.

in spite of myself, is, that this news has been given with modifying statements—we are informed it was a mere 'strategic operation' necessary to the execution of a 'general plan'. The 'operation' in itself seems to me to be a very bad one. . . . I imagined that our only 'plan' was to get 100,000 men together, and to march resolutely against the Germans. . . . Still, I will hope that this is nothing but an idle rumour.

Vallières, in Beauce, Thursday, 8 December

We were beginning to get weary of hearing nothing of the Prussians; at last, yesterday morning, I heard that we were going to give battle. The brigade began to march northwards in sections, with two lines of flankers on the right and left, and we have done two leagues across the fields, now and then hearing a few shots, but seeing nothing.

Our marines have mountain guns, drawn by a single horse, and with a range of 2,000 yards. At twelve o'clock these small pieces were placed in battery in front of the village of Vallières, which we saw a few hundred steps off on our left, and several shots were fired upon enemies whom it was impossible for us to discern; some German shells, too, came and exploded on the fields. At that moment we were halting; some seconds later, the battalion of Mortain was in occupation of Vallières. We sat down in the outhouses, and waited. Strict orders were given that no man was to leave his company.

An hour afterwards we drew up in two parallel columns, at the other end of the village. We were shown the village of Chanteaume, 1,500 yards to the north-west; the Prussians, it was said, were there, and we were going to take it.

We began to move towards it in good order; but we had not gone 500 yards when two or three Chasseurs d'Afrique, who had been sent out as scouts by the general, came back full gallop on their little horses —there was not a single Prussian left in the village. There was nothing more to do but to turn round, and re-enter Vallières.

We passed the night in this wretched place, deserted by almost all its inhabitants, after they had first barricaded their houses. There is not the shadow of an inn to be found; the only grocer has run away, and not a single thing can be got. However, we were fortunate in having had some hours' sleep under a roof—the first time for ten days.

Yesterday there was an uninterrupted booming of cannon all day long on our right, but at a great distance. This morning the concert has begun again much nearer and much louder; they say the battle is along the whole line, from the Loire to this place. Are we at least about to see the decisive day? The battalion of Mortain has some chance of being engaged, as it is placed in the extreme outpost. General du Temple's orders are that 'Major de Grainville is to occupy Vallières, and defend it to the last.'

For these last few days it has been said that the whole of the second army was under the command of the naval captain, Jaurès. Today an order has been read out to the troops, by which General Chanzy is promoted to the rank of general-in-chief of the three corps d'armée. Jaurès will still command the twenty-first. This decree is dated 6 December. The name of Chanzy is entirely unknown to us.

We are quite out of reach of news; since we left Le Mans the only information I have had has been from a scrap of newspaper I found the day before yesterday at La Colombe. It contained a bombastic speech of Gambetta's, announcing General Ducrot's sortie. From the details I have been able to gather, the advantage gained does not seem to me very decided; but still every one appears to be hopeful. . . . One more victory today, and France will, perhaps, be saved!

Friday, 9 December

We have taken root in Vallières. This ignoble village is six leagues from Châteaudun and nine from Orleans. The surrounding country is dull and dreary; at each end of the village, 500 yards out in the plain, stands a windmill, like an outpost sentry, stretching out its great gaunt arms to the four corners of heaven.

Before us are the villages of Chanteaume, Binas, and Marolles; to the right, Saint-Laurent-des-Bois, Villegruau, and farther off, Marché-Noir; behind is the town of Authainville, which we passed through on our way here. We have almost turned our backs on the valley of the Loir.

The battalion of Mortain maintained yesterday an 'expectant attitude', as the papers would say. During the brief hours of daylight this plain of Beauce must have been the scene of great events. The cannonade had begun on our right in the morning; by ten o'clock the thundering was tremendous. We had two companies posted in skirmishing order, in front of our cantonments; they were relieved

every three hours—the position could not have been held longer, for
the cold was piercing, and there having been a slight fall of snow two
days before, our shoes had been converted into icicles. The only
occupation for the unfortunate skirmishers was to listen to the roaring
of the cannon, the shrieking of the *mitrailleuses*,[1] the shrill whistling
of the shells, and the sound, sometimes near and sometimes distant, of
the platoon firing. In vain we strained our eyes to discover what was
passing in the distance; the country, veiled in snow, was blended with
the dull, foggy sky; only now and then, behind the corner of Marolles,
we saw at the distance of a league a jet of flame and white smoke,
announcing the departure of a German ball for some unknown destination. There was little variation in the scene.

The battle did not end till night. During the whole evening sensational reports were flying about, to the effect that the Prussians had
fallen back, leaving the plain covered with dead, and abandoning a
large number of prisoners. Since being a soldier I have begun to be
sceptical; the only fact which appears to me to have any significance
is, that we have slept at Vallières, which I conclude we should not have
done if we had been utterly defeated. Having slept at Vallières is then
a good sign of the times; but, on the other hand, nothing is much more
injurious to the health as being on outpost duty, when one has to pass
the night in a windmill. I prefer even the *tente-abri* to this creaking,
shaking tenement, with the wind coming in through a thousand
chinks and rents. As there is no candle to be had in Vallières, I had to
go up and down the insecure ladders in the dark, groping my way
over planks covered with obstacles, and full of holes large enough to
break one's legs. There could be no question of sleeping; besides, we
were placed there to watch and make observations. At five o'clock I
went out with a patrol to Chanteaume; the greatest terror prevailed
in the village. An old woman called me up into her garret, and made
me count at least forty Uhlans caracoling round a farm a thousand
paces off. 'Save yourself, my boy,' she said, weeping; 'you will only
get killed, and then they will burn down our houses.'

---

[1] The *mitrailleuse* had at the beginning of the war been the French 'secret weapon'. In
size and shape it corresponded to a four-pounder gun. The barrel was a bronzed case
containing twenty-five rifled tubes. The waxed paper cartridges were pre-loaded into a
container in which they were fed *en bloc* into the breech. The twenty-five shots could be
fired either in a ripple or all at once. The maximum rate of fire was 125 shots a minute.
Whilst it was effective if sited to surprise the enemy in close country, it was not when
used as an artillery piece in open battle.

It was broad daylight when we returned, joyful at having found a cup of milk to drink, and three faggots to burn under a wall.

The natives of this country are melancholy specimens of the rustic genus; they are ingeniously selfish and cowardly. Like their neighbours in Perche, they have abjured all idea of devotion to their country; 'patriotism' is a word unknown to them. A very valid train of argument leads them to divide their hatred equally between the Prussians and ourselves; like the Prussians, we are a very troublesome importation, spoilers of their straw and consumers of their fuel. The peasants take no interest in the war, they never wished for it, and they detest it. Besides, it is very doubtful whether the French are more in the right than the Prussians, and whether the God to whom both parties offer up their supplications does not regard us all as being in the wrong. The only thing the Beauceron peasant knows about it is, that here, as everywhere, the innocent suffer for the guilty; the poor man's fields are laid waste, his barn, his hayloft, and his fuel are plundered, and his hens and geese are assassinated in the streets. It is true that, to cover his chief losses, every captain scrupulously hands over to him an order on the commissariat. But he has no confidence in these bits of paper, for which I cannot quite blame him. Often, indeed, he is so absurd as to decline ready money, obeying the instinctive love felt by every small proprietor for his loads of straw and for the trunks of his poplars. It is in vain to assure him that the Germans may come and carry off all he has without paying for anything; he is deaf to our arguments, and buries his stores in his cellars. He has for these two months past been used to the sight of men half dead with cold, hunger, and fatigue; it has ceased to affect him. Everyone in want of anything is looked upon as an enemy—just the reverse of the commercial rule. If all France was like these interesting districts, I know not where we should have found the relics of honour and *amour propre* which has brought together these three hundred thousand men.

Saturday, 10 December

Yesterday—the same as the day before—desperate battle from morning till evening; we heard it, but could see nothing. We have had drill near the windmills. At three o'clock we thought we saw something, and the battalion deployed itself in one line, face to the east. After standing for a few moments in this position, we all went in. As on the day before, we were told of a splendid victory, and the enemy in full retreat. This morning the optimists are triumphant, for we have just received orders to march forward; we are positively leaving Vallières with our arms and baggage, and are going towards the north. The cannonade has begun again on the right, as on these two last days.

Sunday, 11 December

Nothing but one miserable day more added to so many others. From nine o'clock in the morning till nightfall we stood under arms in the fields between Marolles and Vallières. We were expecting every moment our turn to come; it never came. But towards evening we moved two kilometres farther, and we saw a few shells bursting with a great explosion on the frozen ground a hundred paces from our column. Some of the marines were wounded, no one in the battalion of Mortain was touched. At the end of a quarter of an hour we returned; our part was ended for that day, but not our trouble, for, on re-entering Vallières, we found our cantonments occupied by a battalion of the line. We had to storm for an hour, and at last appeal to the general, before we could get our quarters restored to us. The officers of the line affect great contempt for the Mobiles; but they have no occasion to be prouder than we are.

This morning all is silence on the plain; one would suppose that all was over. We are on the move, and our orders are to hold ourselves in readiness for any emergency. But what strikes me as singular is that there is no further mention of victory, and of marching to the front; only of 'good results', 'satisfactory days', and 'turning movements'. All this is very indefinite, and sounds to me anxious; however, we must not anticipate the worst. The cold is less severe, and in some places the snow is melting.

To La Comtesse de Rougé

Vallières, 11 December 1870

Madame,

I write to you as I do to my own people, without pen, ink, or table, and on whatever sort of paper I can contrive to get possession of.

Fernand will have told you that I have not at all given up our diary, as you might have believed. The little notebook will contain some pages that will be historical. All we have seen, done, said, or felt since the retreat from Nogent will remain for ever engraven on our memory. The day will come, I hope, when we may be able to talk it over with you by the fireside, if you will allow us.

Fernand and I are amongst those who are best able to withstand the fatigues and miseries of a soldier's life. If fire and sword leave us standing, I scarcely think that cold, or weariness, or want will overpower us.

We all grieve deeply over Christian de Failly's absence. We have had no news of him, and we greatly fear that he is seriously ill.

We have been for these three last days quartered in the little village of Vallières; there has been fighting all the time, but we cannot learn what the result has been. Yesterday there was a loud cannonade and musketry fire from morning till evening, and we passed nearly the whole day under arms, in the fields covered with rime, waiting our turn, which never came. Towards evening we were made to advance a little farther, and we had the satisfaction of seeing a few shells bursting on the frozen furrows. We had no wounded in our battalion; a shell exploded near a column that was marching 100 paces from us on the left, and caused a terrible confusion, but not many men appear to have been struck. The course which a shell takes is comparatively slow; the soldiers hear its whistle in the distance, and as it grows louder the number of those who throw themselves on the ground increases; in about four or five seconds the thunderclap is heard, clouds of dust and smoke begin to fly, and the men rise and hasten to exchange experiences.

At dusk we all re-entered Vallières. As on every other evening, there was nothing heard of but 'complete victory', 'innumerable prisoners', and 'the enemy in full retreat'. What is certain is that we have kept our positions, dined by our own fireside, and slept upon our own straw, and this morning the cannon is heard only at rare intervals. It is now one o'clock, and it is less and less likely that we shall have to move today.

The valley of the Loir, which we have passed through since leaving Vendôme, is one of the most charming parts of France; but we were so sad, so disheartened, and the cold was so intense that everything looked to us desolate and miserable.

Adieu, madame, and *au revoir* I trust. I cannot believe that all this will last much longer. We shall, please God, have patience and good fortune enough to see the end of our sufferings, We think of those who are at a distance, and who are kind enough to remember us, and from our inmost hearts we send them our respect and our affection, a large share of which, as far as I am concerned, will be for yourself and Monsieur de Rougé.

Courcillon, near Fréteval, Wednesday, 14 December, evening

We can no longer have any doubt—all is again lost. What passed during those four days at Vallières? Not one of us knows, but the result is too apparent; it is retreat—last night it was rout. I may say that I have taken part in a great modern battle, and yet I have nothing to relate concerning it; in this age nations destroy each other without coming face to face: . . . where is the mêlée of ancient times? I had always thought that 200,000 Frenchmen in the open field would be stronger than all the German hordes. Who can tell us why we are here? But it is in vain to make conjectures.

During the day of the 11th alarming reports came one after another; the whole night we were kept on the alert, and the following morning we expected every moment to start. Where to? We had no idea. I ventured, however, to hope that at all events our new march would not take us farther from Paris; and when at eleven o'clock the order sounded, 'put on your knapsacks', we were not quite reduced to despair. But on leaving the town, one glance over the plain destroyed our last illusions; the whole brigade was taking the road to Authainville—we were turning our backs upon the field of battle.

We put off all inquiries till later on—we could think of nothing for the moment but how to get our feet out of the thick mud through which we had to march at the quickest pace. The frost was gone, and it was a complete thaw. We arrived at Authainville quite out of breath; half a league over such ground had done for us. We had to encamp. The mire was so deep that no pickets would stand; we found a little straw to lay under the tents, but the water oozed through it as soon as we attempted to lean upon it. That night was a very suffering one for the troops.

I had availed myself of a moment's respite to speak to some of the officers. I heard with consternation that the Prussians were close to Blois and Vendôme, and that we were retreating for fear of being

attacked in the rear. 'But the battle?' I said; 'the battle then is lost?'
The answer was that the battle had remained undecided; but that the
enemy had suffered enormous losses, and that we must not despair. . . .
Our instructions were to be satisfied; there was nothing more to be
said. . . . I asked myself if the whole world had gone mad.

What, in my ignorance of tactics, I could not comprehend, was
that we should be turned and intercepted, when, the seat of war
being in France, we had placed ourselves, with a large and almost
unscathed army, between the frontier and the enemy. . . . They had
not 'turned', happy fellows! . . . O that I had the dictionary of the
Academy to study there the different meanings of that fatal word
'turn'.

The next morning we set out again, marching towards the Loir.
This new retreat had no resemblance to that of Thiron; instead of
hurrying on in breathless haste we moved with the greatest delibera-
tion, which was quite as fatiguing. Constant halts, when one has to
keep standing the whole time, only make one's knapsack feel heavier.
Besides, as the enemy was not far off, it was necessary to have a line of
flankers marching 300 yards from the roadside, parallel with the
column. These unfortunate flankers having instructions to keep always
on a level with their respective battalions, were forced sometimes to
march at a gymnastic pace, and sometimes to stop short in fields which
the thaw had converted into oceans of mud—sticky, unfathomable
mud, in which the foot sank ankle deep, and came out again loaded
with heavy, icy clay. The country was very hilly; they had to be
incessantly descending and reascending the hollows of the ground,
whilst the brigade followed the straight and horizontal road. From
time to time firing was heard in the woods on the left, telling us that
the enemy was threatening in good earnest to overtake us.

Each company had to supply this service of flankers for two hours.
We did not arrive at Morée till sunset; it had taken us the whole day
to do ten kilometres; from the fatigue we felt, it might have been ten
leagues.

We did not stop a single instant at Morée, but pushed on straight
to Fréteval, where we expected to encamp as we had done the night
before. Till then we had marched in tolerable order; but on the road
to Fréteval there was a frightful crush. The superior officers were not
agreed apparently as to their respective places in the column. As none
of them would give way, it was impossible to advance; if we made
ten or twelve steps we had to come to a standstill for a quarter of an

hour or more. Night, when it fell, found us hemmed in between the hillside and an interminable artillery train, whose officers were disputing their passage with the hussars and dragoons. Every now and then the axles creaked, and we thought they were moving; but no, when they had gone half a dozen steps they made a fresh halt, of which it was impossible to foresee the end. With the closing darkness had come on a pouring rain, which lasted the whole night. As we could see nothing, it was hopeless to think of looking for a dry corner to lean against; the banks were trickling with innumerable muddy rivulets, that came dropping into the ruts. Some of the men, however, discovered a sort of cavern that was half flooded, but where they succeeded in lighting a few sticks, and in securing a moment's cheerfulness round the fire.

This lasted from five o'clock till nine. On entering Fréteval we learnt that we were to encamp farther on, in a wood at the top of the hill. We resigned ourselves to our fate; for it was evident there was no room in the village, and perhaps we might find some dry places under the fir-trees; at any rate, we should be able to make a fire. We, therefore, courageously climbed the hill on which stands the tower of Fréteval; the road was full of quagmires, so treacherous that you did not suspect their existence till you suddenly found yourself sinking into them up to your waist. I was fortunate enough to avoid such catastrophes. When we reached the top it was impossible to discover the wood which had been assigned to us. The major made an attempt to get into the fields, but his horse sank in the mire, and he had great difficulty in regaining the road. All this time the rain kept pouring down. The officers had to announce to the men that there was no other place for them to spend the night in but the roadside.

The limits of human strength and patience were exceeded; the retreat had produced its inevitable moral effect, and no hope, no thought of their country now sustaining them any longer, every man began to think of himself. 'Come,' said one of the fellows to his comrade, 'we two will make off alone to Vendôme. It will be all in our way.' 'Who will go with me to Le Mans?' murmured another. I asked myself whether an officer could in conscience take down the names of these men, and have them arrested as deserters. For my part, I could not undertake to do so. I encouraged those around to have patience, since we were marching towards Normandy, where we should no doubt be disbanded; and then I clambered up the banks in search of a resting place.

The sound of the major's voice calling to us gave me the energy necessary to get out of a bog into which I had fallen on my way from a farmhouse, where I had found every corner occupied. When I got back to the road again I heard that the whole battalion was going down to the railway-station to receive some rations of bread, and that afterwards every one was to find such quarters as he could. Those who had not strayed too far answered to the summons. We retraced our steps down the hill, and we had the happiness of finding a wagon laden with bread, which we immediately plundered. A rendezvous was given for seven the next morning on a small esplanade at the entrance of the village. After having knocked in vain at a great many doors, I found at midnight a corner of refuge in an inn-parlour. We wrapped ourselves up, my friend and myself, in a rug we possessed, and we slept five hours amongst franc-tireurs, Mobiles from every corps, soldiers of the line, men from the north and from the south, whom fortune had crowded together on the same floor.

This morning we recrossed the Loir, and scaled the opposite heights. We are resting in a little hamlet belonging to a commune whose name I do not know; before us is the tower of Fréteval; behind us the great forest of the Duke of Doudeauville.

Four or five men out of each company have disappeared. Many, who did not hear the last order, were left behind on the hill, under some tree or hedge; those who went off to Vendôme are supposed to have been taken prisoners.

Friday, 16 December

Two more days of fighting, of which we have been inactive spectators. We thought we should have rested on Wednesday. Our hopes were doomed to be disappointed; at twelve we had to put on our knapsacks, and take up fighting positions along the road to Paris. The mud, swelled by the deluge of rain that had fallen, was greasy and deep; we sank slowly into it, hardly able to maintain our balance; there was not a single dry spot in the field on which we could sit down or even lay our knapsacks. We had to be incessantly changing from one foot to the other to keep ourselves from sinking up to our knees; this exercise lasted four hours. Our only pastime was listening to the cannonade, and watching the firing of our guns, which were placed in battery 300 yards from where we stood. This day was, I imagine, without any result. We were told, as usual, that the Prussians had been repulsed; but we were becoming incredulous.

The next day, 15 December, we started at nine o'clock, and retraced our steps along the Paris road, which we had gone over the morning before. The battalion was posted in a hollow of the ground, where the soil was less wet than elsewhere. The men were allowed to sit down, to set their knapsacks on the ground, and to make their soup; the vine-poles serving, as usual, for fuel. On the summit of the hill a few guns were placed which answered the Prussians' fire.

For the first time for many days there was a little sunshine, and the air was mild; we stretched some rugs over the damp grass, and passed a tolerably tranquil day. I endeavoured to get some explanation of our incomprehensible retreat; but no one could tell me anything. It was even said that General du Temple was in ignorance of the reason, and was as much dismayed as ourselves. He is reported to have proposed during those days of Vallières, to go to the front, to have a nearer view of the enemy; and the story adds further that the generals-in-chief considered it too dangerous a proposition to be entertained, and that it was best to wage war with our cannon at the greatest possible distance. We have, they say, consumed 15,000 cartridges—I doubt whether we have destroyed 15,000 enemies. It is not to be supposed that the naval captain, Jaurès, and the cavalry officer, Guyon, are wanting in courage; besides, they have their orders; but I fear that Reichshoffen, Sedan, and Metz have made the French unlearn the great art of daring.

General du Temple dares, both for himself and for us; he has great confidence in his marines, and esteem for the Norman Mobiles, and we are very grateful to him. When all the corps d'armée had passed the Loir, it was found that amongst other things that had been forgotten, the bridge of Fréteval had not been destroyed. To repair this little omission we had to carry the village by storm. Our general sent his marines, who executed his orders faithfully; but not without losing a number of men from the musketry fire kept up by the enemy under shelter of the houses. This pretty feat of arms was achieved yesterday at dusk, just as we were quitting our positions to return to our cantonments.

For our quarters last night we have had a nest of three or four filthy cottages, known in the neighbourhood by the name of Lanerie. It is a 1,000 paces from Courcillon, which was occupied by other troops. The three first companies had to encamp.

Yesterday I had to exchange by order of the major, and take command of the fourth, in which there is not a single officer left.

This morning there was a distribution of some articles of camp-equipage, and forty infantry *capotes* [capes]. But the fields of Beauce have already given our unhappy Mobiles bronchial and rheumatic affections, from which many will never recover.

Today we hear scarcely any firing; it is four o'clock; no doubt we shall rest till tomorrow.

Mondoubleau, Sunday, 18 December

I had just closed this notebook, when I perceived an orderly officer galloping towards us along the muddy road; he was bringing the order for our immediate departure. We took the road to Paris; but we foresaw we should not follow it long, and in a quarter of an hour the column turned to the left, by a cross-road which led us into the heart of the forest. The last glimmerings of daylight disappeared in the dark thicket, and the retreat continued, sometimes with the most hopeless slowness, sometimes with such rapidity that we could not keep up, and interrupted by interminable halts. By nine o'clock we had scarcely gone two leagues; the rain had been falling incessantly since sunset. We passed by the gates of La Gaudinière; that beautiful mansion, now transformed into a hospital, was wrapped in darkness and silence. At ten o'clock we saw the last of the tall trees. We heard we were going to Ville-aux-Clercs, a large town a league and a half farther on.

Gambetta had issued a circular ordering the generals to make the troops encamp only when no room could be found for them in the houses;[1] we therefore hoped that when we had once got out of the forest, and left the enemy behind us, our miseries would be a little mitigated. The beau-ideal of happiness appeared to the half-sleeping soldiers to be a barn full of straw, a great heap of faggots, and a peasant selling cider on his doorstep. But after passing through Ville-aux-Clercs without halting, we had to summon up our courage for another league. The sight of the little village of Romilly, where the division was to take up its quarters, brought us back to stern reality; the first houses we passed showed us that all were full, and that the

[1] Up until this time it was the Prussians who had enjoyed the warmth and security of houses. The French themselves had been expected to camp in the open.

fate of the last-comers must be to sleep under the open sky. The major hastened to dismiss the men, so as to give them a chance of finding some corner still unoccupied. The next day we set forth again at eight o'clock, in great confusion; the companies could not be reformed till we had gone more than a league's distance; many of the men had gone on in front, and were waiting for us by the roadside. . . .

Yesterday at twelve o'clock we left the cross-roads, which we had followed since Fréteval, to take the road to Mondoubleau. The rain had ceased, and we marched at a good pace; we even resumed some little gaiety. General Guyon, too, was in good spirits; he passed down the column, telling us kindly that we should soon be at Mondoubleau, and that if the men were not too much fatigued, we should push on to Le Mans, where we should have a few days' rest. We wished for nothing better; from the moment we had given up the hope of marching to Paris, Le Mans had become the goal of all our desires.

At the end of an hour we began to descend into the valley of Mondoubleau; we passed through the principal streets of the town, and at the outskirts we reached the lowest level where flows the river Graisne. Passing over it by a handsome bridge, we came into a damp pasture-land, stretching out towards the south between steep hills; this opening leads to the Loir, then to the fields of Touraine. The eye begins to see visions of the south.

Having come to the bottom of the valley, we re-ascend on the other side, and, turning round, we behold one of the loveliest corners of the Maine. At sunset the little town, the old castle, and the beautiful leaning tower are bathed in golden light, whilst the more distant hills are turned into blue and rose-coloured mountains; at our feet the river, the poplars, and the great buildings of the tanyard are already lost in mist and darkness. Whilst we were gazing at this view, the tents were being pitched all over the hillside; after a halt of three hours, it had been decided we were to encamp. The crowd and confusion were frightful; part of the 16 Corps was retreating by that road; the town, exhausted by requisitions, and inundated by German and French troops in turn, had nothing left to offer us.

At this moment all the tide of men, carriages, and cannons which have passed the night in the valley, are crowded together in a narrow pass, by which we are to go to Semur or Connerré. The battalion has been for a good hour under arms, but the brigade du Temple has scarcely begun to set itself in motion; we shall not be on our way till noon.

Pont-de-Gênes, near Montfort-le-Rotrou, Tuesday, 20 December

From Mondoubleau to Semur it is only four leagues; but our march was so slow and so often interrupted, that we did not arrive till midnight, and we were as much worn out as if we had made a long day's journey. The country we passed through was full of lovely and varied prospects; there is nothing magnificent, all is small, peaceful, and smiling; the rivers are slender, the valleys narrow and deep; the woods during the summer season must be delicious. In the mild weather it is now, we begin to dream, in the best hours of the day, of spring, and of the end of all these calamities.

We came through several pretty villages, of which I do not know the name. It seems that the enemy is not very distant from this fair country. The night before last we had to supply the outposts, and the strictest vigilance is observed. It has been a severe night.

Yesterday we started at nine o'clock, and passed through Semur, encamping behind the town. A march of disheartening slowness brought us to the village of Thorigné only after dark, though we had scarcely gone three leagues. The column was drawn up a quarter of a league farther on, and it was announced to the men, who had neither meat nor bread left, that they might make their soup. There was a distribution, however, or rather some railway-wagons were plundered; but our battalion got nothing, and the men were in despair. At nine that same evening we had to start again; most of the men had had nothing to eat. Those who were in command of the column took this opportunity of making us accelerate our speed, and for three hours we marched in breathless haste. We passed through Connerré almost at a run. Many of the men, overpowered with fatigue and hunger, could go no farther, and went and knocked at the doors; on all sides arose murmurs so well founded that the officers felt they could not notice them with any great severity. When at midnight we arrived at Pont-de-Gênes there were at least twenty-five missing in every company. This morning we are resting till twelve o'clock, and then we start for Yvré-l'Evêque. We are not, it seems, to go to Le Mans, the troops are to be quartered in the surrounding villages; perhaps, instead of the rest so long promised, we are to sustain another cruel disappointment. We have had no food given out, and there is none to be found anywhere. The men are besieging the bakers' shops. The commanding officers have posted sentries round the ovens, who are in great danger of being cut to pieces; several collisions have already taken place, and I have seen blood flowing. If anything is to be left of the Second Army of the Loire, it is quite time we should get to the end of this retreat.

Coulaines, near Le Mans, Thursday, 22 December, morning

If a few days' rest are to be granted to us we shall spend them in this wretched little village, buried in a hollow, near the high road to Alençon. This is the 'Lieu dit l'Ardoise', belonging to the commune of Coulaines, an important suburb of Le Mans. This promised land, for which we have sighed so long, presented yesterday afternoon a scene of mournful desolation.

We had come from Yvré-l'Evêque, where, after a march of four leagues across the Maine *bocage*, we had found detestable quarters, and very indifferent rations. A large number of troops having already passed this way the resources of the country were exhausted and the inhabitants deeply dejected. They had learnt to know the thousand miseries involved by the presence of the troops, and they cast despairing looks at their gardens given up to pillage and their half demolished stacks of fuel. In the house where part of my company is lodged the room was crammed with soldiers, the hearth was invaded, the table taken possession of, the beds covered with sabres and knapsacks. A poor woman sat rocking her sick child, weeping over it, and saying she wished it might die, and be safe from the miseries of this world. I tried to comfort her; but our men were objects also of the deepest compassion—after the hard campaign they had just gone through, they find themselves condemned to these wretched quarters, where they can only sleep under shelter on condition of being literally piled up one upon the other. To make our position still more agreeable, we are today to be on outpost duty, and the night will be passed under the stars in the park belonging to a château which bears the sweet name of 'Chêne-de-Coeur' [Heart's Oak]. We must not think of Le Mans before tomorrow; till then we must content ourselves with the sight of the cathedral tower, which is three-quarters of a league from us. But they tell us that when the guard is relieved, leave of absence will be granted: we shall be able to get some shoes and clothing, to have our hair cut, and to dine at the table d'hôte; we shall see our friends, we shall get the papers, and those who have time to read them may perhaps be able to tell us what we have been doing in Beauce. A few moments spent in the civilised world again will, indeed, do us a great deal of good.

Coulaines, 26 December

Our quarters at Coulaines are decidedly not unbearable, especially now that we are not compelled to remain in them from morning till night. Officers and men get leave easily to go into the town. And besides, on our return from outpost duty last Friday, we found that other lodgings were assigned to us, where we are far more comfortable. The men are beginning to recover themselves a little; it seems probable that we shall not move again for several days. One night more we shall spend in the woods of Chêne-de-Coeur; and though it has begun to freeze again *à pierre fendre*, it will not be a worse place to encamp in than any other; we shall have plenty of straw, water, and fuel. If this post is to be kept any length of time, all the wood in M. Augier's park will fall beneath the hatchets of our Mobiles, and there will be a fine view from the road of Sarthe, the railway, and the opposite heights of Saint-Saturnin, over which those who have lively imaginations are perpetually fancying they see the Prussians approaching. . . .

Yesterday (Christmas Day) General du Temple reviewed us at noon, in a stinging frost. He can now bear witness to the fact that, thanks to the care of the administration, the men are in rags, and have to march very nearly bare-footed. We are informed, however, that there are going to be important distributions of shoes and clothing; and it is true that some dozens of red trousers have already arrived.

The 30th Marching Regiment is, I hear, to be reorganised. Colonel Lemoine-Desmares is absent on account of his health, and our major, M. de Grainville, is to be appointed in his place.

On Friday I went again to Le Mans; the place is inundated with troops; the surrounding villages are equally overflowing; altogether we have more than a hundred thousand men there.

The capital of the Maine has become a general rendezvous, not only for the army, but for all who have friends or relations under our flag; they avail themselves of these few days' respite to come and see them. The shopkeepers are all agreed in asking double price for everything one cannot do without, and thanks to the misfortunes of their country, are making very substantial gains; but it must not be forgotten that the billeting of the troops upon them is a very serious evil. And yet how far more are the country people to be pitied, who lose everything and sell hardly anything.

For anyone passing down the high street of Le Mans or the Place des Halles, the town would appear as gay, as animated, and as glittering with gold and pleasure as any country town could be. There are no indications here of the misery and suffering which prevail in the more distant quarters. Many diseases, especially the small-pox, are making terrible ravages in the hospitals; the sick have not enough straw even to keep them from freezing, nor sufficient soup to save them from dying of hunger. The charity of the ladies of Le Mans, inexhaustible as it is, is still inadequate for the relief of all these miseries. During this campaign, in which we have not had a single man wounded, our effectives have been reduced from 130 to 115, and they will certainly be reduced lower still. Forced marches, privations, nights passed in the open air without rugs or greatcoats, are producing their fatal consequences. We hear that the Prussians are suffering also greatly from various infectious diseases.

The staff officers have established themselves in the theatre, on the Place des Jacobins. It is there that our 'passes' are countersigned when we wish to go into the town; it is there that we saw the other day a captain dragged along by four soldiers, because he was unable to produce a *laissez-passer*.

The military police here is the most absurd and ridiculous institution that can be conceived. The officers and men are strictly prohibited from going into the town without a 'pass', covered with half a dozen signatures, and as many stamps. But as there is no real guard established in the suburbs, and no regular surveillance in the town, not unfrequently these 'passes' are sold by one to another, or they are dispensed with altogether, and generally without detection; if the culprit, however, is discovered, he is sure to be treated as if he was the worst of vagabonds. . . . The regulation is that every café must close exactly at nine o'clock, and the order is punctually obeyed. Everywhere the lights are put out at the same moment, and the doors of the public resorts give egress to a motley, noisy throng, who are soon driven from further ramblings by the fear of cold and of patrols, and all sinks into silence.

The papers which are published every evening by the Le Mans editors are seized upon with the most eager impatience. We find in them all sorts of different opinions on the 'situation', romantic narratives of the war, plans of the campaign found on lawyers' notebooks, but facts there are few or none. The occupation of Rouen, on 4 December, by Manteuffel, however, cannot be concealed. Up to the 20th of this month we had no suspicion of this fatal blow, the success of which is due most probably to our retreat. Tours is also in the hands of the enemy, and the Government has fled to Bordeaux. All I hear, and all I read, increases the indignation I felt when I left Vallières against those who are entrusted with the direction of this way. What is the scheme proposed now that Paris is abandoned, and that the enemy is in possession of the Loire? France has too much self-love to confess herself vanquished, and not enough heroism to make any supreme sacrifice for the sake of victory.

To drive out the stranger or perish, that is the official programme; to march, to fight as long as the struggle lasts, and, above all, not to be the first to say that one is weary of it, that is the thought which is in each separate breast. Now we hear of a march to Paris, of a decisive battle. As if it could ever be easier to march to Paris than it was three weeks ago! As if even a victory could save us! The First Army of the Loire, under General d'Aurelle, has melted away in Sologne, no one knows how. Those who love to deceive themselves say that Bourbaki has led it into Germany, and that in the north General Faidherbe is at the head of a large body of troops. God grant that it might be so! After all, the Prussians must be greatly reduced; we hear that they are decimated by the small-pox, and no one can say exactly what is the strength of either party. . . .

Coulaines, Tuesday, 3 January 1871

Le Mans is the most agreeable country town I ever was in. I have found there for a second time, on returning from Beauce, the most affectionate reception from relations whom I had never seen a month before. When we were at the end of our terrible retreat from Nogent we were at the last gasp from weariness; the town was blocked up with troops, and to find a bed was considered to be impossible. I then remembered that I could not be a perfect stranger in this town, which I was entering for the first time under circumstances so extraordinary, and I bethought myself of asking a citizen who was passing by which was the way to the Hôtel de Montesson. I rang—not without misgivings—at the great gates that had been pointed out to me, and no sooner had I crossed the threshold than I congratulated myself upon my courage. I found myself welcomed as a son of the house. The day after I presented myself at the house of my cousin, the Dowager Marquise de Montesson. She received me with much affection, and spoke of the two invasions she had witnessed sixty years ago. I passed on that occasion three nights under this venerable roof, to which I have now come once again for shelter. My cousin is ill; the sorrows of her country, of her friends, and of her family, have cast a gloom over her beautiful old age. One of her grandsons is a prisoner in Germany; the other, Charles de Montesson, has been languishing for two months in the Château de la Gaudinière, where a severe wound keeps him in captivity. There are other Montessons also in the army, as captains of Mobiles or orderly officers. All the Le Mans nobility rose at the same instant. Some of the young men just mounted their horses and joined the battalion of Zouaves under Couëssin, acting as scouts. Every lady in Le Mans makes lint, and takes her part in nursing the sick and wounded. Every one here does what he can for the common cause. The Bordeaux people ought to come to Le Mans to learn that there is something better for them to do than to scream and to vociferate.

When our duty calls us away from this dear town, our thoughts will remain here with our friends. Monsieur and Madame de Rougé, and Madame de Grainville arrived a few days ago. The Boule d'Or, where they are staying, has become a most fashionable resort. Madame de Tocqueville is there, making a collection for the wounded, and enlivening with her sprightliness and wit the little dinners given by our superior officers. Our major is celebrating his promotion, for he has just been appointed lieutenant-colonel of the 30th Marching Regiment, and he has invited me to celebrate my own, having proposed me as captain of the fourth company. I have been acting as such for the last three weeks. We hear that General Guyon, who was in command of our division, has been replaced by General de Villeneuve; for us it is one name instead of another, and nothing more.

The weather continues icy cold. We drill at Coulaines morning and evening. M. de Graville de Mailly, formerly officer of the line, and captain of our second company, has been promoted to the rank of major, and is to replace M. de Grainville. We all love and respect this brave old warrior, and shall obey him with our whole heart. But we cannot think without sadness of the time when we shall have to depart for some other destination, and our colonel and his faithful officers

will be separated by a great distance. When shall we leave this place—
and what are we going to do?

The dissipation in which we have been living during these last few
days has prevented us from asking ourselves this question, and if we
did we could give no answer. Sometimes I reproach myself for my
lightheartedness, and, returning to an old habit of my youth, I begin
to reflect. Since we have been here our spirits have greatly revived; I
can scarcely say why. The only good news we have had has been the
capture of 100 Germans near Vendôme. Paris is more closely besieged
than ever, and we hear nothing from the north. But rest and enliven-
ment have had their usual effects; in spite of ourselves, we are still
animated by a lingering spark of hope, and we now speak very coolly
of a rumour which had at first caused great excitement. There had been
a question, it appears, of sending back the battalions of La Manche to
the Carentan lines. We thought that as we have been made to march
up and down Beauce for a month to avoid fighting we might just as
well have sat still. But we are evidently thinking of making one more
effort, for all the available troops are being assembled, and an attempt
is being made to reorganise them. Képis, jackets, a few *capotes* and
red trousers have been given to the men; they begin to look themselves
again, and to assume quite a martial appearance. We too have been
buying cloaks, boots, and belts, and are once more well equipped. For
my part, I desire passionately to have another sight of the Germans,
and to have some opportunity of doing honour to my third stripe.
We know nothing whatever of their movements; on the south they
do not seem to have got beyond Tours, and on this side they are not
considered to be very near.

Friday, 6 January

Nothing new. This life might go on for some time without our
finding it wearisome. All the pleasantest people in France are congre-
gating in Le Mans; we have had the joy of seeing M. and Mme de
Beauffort and their son Louis, who is orderly officer to Admiral
Jauréguiberry, and greatly distinguished himself at one of the battles
in Beauce.

A mournful procession passed through this town the other day on
its road to Sablé—the honoured remains of the Duc de Luynes. They
had been at last recovered; and his mother, the Duchesse de Chevreuse,
wished them to be borne to a distance from those battlefields which

were the scenes of German triumphs. Charles de Luynes was twenty-six years of age; he had been married three years, and has left a son and a daughter.[1]

General de Villeneuve has passed the division in review on the high road to Ballon; he also assembled the officers, and inquired of each major what he was most in want of for his men. The unanimous answer was—shoes! This part of the military attire, like many other things in France, has fallen into a state of deplorable decay.

Many reports are flying about; but we pay little attention to them. The cold weather continued.

---

[1] A word here to the memory of Charles de Luynes, who gave up life so gallantly to his country, and whose sainted mother and young widow stand foremost amongst the victims of this unhappy war. Every brilliant or happy thing which this world can afford seemed to have been lavished upon the Duc de Luynes — master, at the age of twenty-two, of one of the largest territorial possessions in France, including the princely residence of Dampierre, the castles of Luynes, Châteaudun, and many others. He had been married, in December 1867, to his cousin, Mademoiselle de la Rochefoucauld, descended from Hortense de Luynes, Duchesse Matthieu de Montmorency, and their union, the result of a mutual attachment, was happy in every respect. The Duc de Luynes, who was killed at Sougy, had distinguished himself by his great intrepidity at the battle of Coulmiers, where his only brother, Paul de Chevreuse, volunteer at the age of nineteen, received in the foot a wound so severe that it nearly maimed him for life. Almost all the fair country that was drenched with some of the best blood of France, in the contest between the Germans and the armies of the Loire, had belonged to their ancestors, and was theirs still for the most part. The forest of Marchénoir had been their father's favourite hunting resort, and like the knights of old they fell, one never to rise again, fighting with their own men on their own land. [Roger de Mauni.]

V

The Loss of Le Mans

On New Year's Day, 1871, Prince Frederick Charles received the order to march to the west. On 6 January, four German Corps began their concentric advance on Le Mans. By the 10th, in spite of the appalling weather and the resistance of Chanzy's columns, they were within a few miles of the town. For the whole of that day their attack was held, while Chanzy summoned up his last reserves, which included every able-bodied man on whom he could lay his hands. The attack was held again on the 11th, until in the evening the Tenth Prussian Corps, which had been delayed *en route*, made its appearance on the French right flank, on the opposite side of the town from where Roger de Mauni found himself. The Prussians were exhausted and the attack they launched carried no great force, but by chance it fell on the sector defended by some of Chanzy's weakest and most ill-equipped troops, the Brittany Mobiles. They broke and ran, abandoning their trenches and earthworks which protected the French right. In vain General Jauréguiberry tried to retake the position; the troops he collected melted away in the dark before they could be brought into action. Finally, after midnight, he was forced to counsel retreat. Chanzy bowed to the inevitable, but even so held his position long enough for most of the stores accumulated in the town to be evacuated. The Germans entered and set fire to Le Mans at 2.30 p.m. on 12 January.

Chanzy directed the retreat through Alençon, where he intended to reform the army. The Germans were too exhausted to pursue energetically, though Roger de Mauni had dealings with a few of them on the way. Chanzy believed that with a reconstituted force he would be capable of marching towards Paris once again, but even Gambetta could not accept the likelihood of this and counselled further withdrawal to the west, to Laval. Here, for the next few weeks until the final armistice, Chanzy devoted his prodigious energy and organising ability to recreating the Second Army of the Loire. Further north, Faidherbe, too, after a brief success at Bapaume on 3 January, had by the end of the month been forced back on the defensive into the fortress area on the Belgian border.

Great as had been the efforts on the left wing, it was to the right that Gambetta and de Freycinet looked for a real victory. It will be remembered that General Bourbaki, with the First Army of the Loire, had been sent to the Saône valley to relieve the siege of Belfort and to cut the Prussian lines of communication. By 5 January, the force had arrived in the east after a hideous train journey, which in many cases had involved troops spending up to ten days in unheated carriages in temperatures of ten to fifteen degrees below zero centigrade. By the 14th Bourbaki was in a position to threaten relief of the siege of Belfort, but his movement had been so slow and indecisive that the enemy had had time to form a defensive line along the river Lisaine. After a three-day battle he was forced to withdraw, but by this time his line of retreat was cut off by additional German forces which had hurried to the scene across the plateau of Langres. On the 22nd, Bourbaki was at Besançon, and by the 24th had decided that his only hope of safety was to make for Pontarlier in the Jura where he might possibly slip away along the Swiss frontier. On the 26th he tried to commit suicide, and failed. His successor was left to negotiate with the Swiss the convention which allowed the remains of the army to pass into internment across the frontier at Château Joux. Even today the term 'l'armée de Bourbaki' is used in France to describe disastrous military confusion.

Back in Paris, after the failure of the great sortie at the beginning of December, there had been one minor attempt at a break-out to the north at a time when it was felt that Faidherbe was gaining some success. This was on the 21st of the month, when an attack had been launched towards Le Bourget. It had petered out in the frozen fields, overwhelmed by artillery fire and with the attackers hardly gaining a sight of the opposing infantry. Then, on 5 January, had begun the bombardment of the city.

Reading Roger de Mauni's account, and looking at a history of the war, one gains the impression of an almost unrelieved series of French failures and disasters. This was so. But on the other side as well, in the German camp, there was grave dissatisfaction at the way the war was being conducted. On two occasions German General Headquarters had been ready to evacuate Versailles in response to imagined threats from Paris or the Army of the Loire, and all the time the High Command was anxiously sensitive to the vulnerability of the lines of communication to the east whereby the armies around Paris were supported. Von Moltke had promised the fall of Paris in not more than a week or two from the beginning of the siege. It was now over 100 days since the encirclement was complete and still the capital held out and still new armies formed in the provinces. The bombardment, agreed to only after much argument, was an attempt to solve the deadlock. It was, in fact, a failure. The casualties inflicted and the material damage caused had been small; the psychological effect was to raise a wave of sympathy for the Parisians throughout Europe and to increase their determination to resist. It was partly this determination and partly the fear of revolution felt by the authorities that led the military commander in Paris to countenance a final attempt at mass break-out. The attack was launched on 19 January towards Bougival in the direction of Versailles by a force of 90,000 men, at least half of whom were National Guard. It was a complete failure. Worse, it happened at the same moment as news arrived of Chanzy's loss of Le Mans and with the realisation that starvation was only just around the corner. On 23 January Jules Favre set out for Versailles to seek for terms.

On the 28th an armistice was signed to come into force immediately in Paris and in the rest of France in three days' time. It was to last until 19 February. During this time, facilities would be given for a National Assembly to be elected to meet at Bordeaux to decide whether and on what terms peace should be made. A balloonist was dispatched to Bordeaux to give the Delegation the news, but whether by accident or deliberately he overflew the coast and disappeared for ever into the Atlantic. As a result Gambetta did not hear of the capitulation of Paris until the 29th and did not receive the terms of the armistice until the 31st. When he did, he accepted them only as a chance to train and re-equip the armies to continue the struggle. At the same time he published eloquent decrees designed to ensure the election of an Assembly of like mind to himself. A meeting of the Republican party was called at Bordeaux. Resolutions were passed declaring that the capitulation was not binding on the Provinces. Gambetta was invited to become head of a Committee of Public Safety to act independently of the Paris government. The situation had almost reached the point where Paris was prepared to put an end to the authority of the Delegation, when, on 8 February, Gambetta resigned. Although he still personally believed that the war should continue, he was not prepared to push his point of view to the extent of a breach with the accredited government.

And indeed the elections showed that he would have been wrong. Although Paris and the large cities returned deputies of the left, the Assembly which was elected proved to be predominantly conservative. Thiers, who since the fall of Metz had been publicly advocating peace at any price, received the largest personal support of any and was chosen to head the peace negotiations.

This was a sad end to the hopes which those at Le Mans had held only six weeks before.

Le Mans, Sunday, 8 January, 11 p.m.

At last we are on the move, and this time we hope it is to fight. When we arrived here three weeks ago, we were in the lowest state of discouragement and depression; now we are full of ardent desire to try our fate once more. I will not believe that all is lost. General Bourbaki is reported to be seriously threatening Germany. Trochu, with his 200,000 men, may well do something. . . . And we? We are more than 100,000, and are in a very strong position. . . . Must we absolutely despair of having our own good day? It is true that at the point we have reached, one victory would not rid us of the invaders. . . . But this nation is so strong! . . . If once a little real enthusiasm were to enter into it, nothing would seem impossible. For the moment let us do our best to defend this dear, this charming town, where we have met with so much kindness. Except our own, I know of no province in France so generous, so hospitable, so patriotic as the Maine.

It was at five o'clock p.m. that we received the news we had been expecting for some days. 'The Germans are approaching.' The note transmitted by the staff states that 'possibly the 21 Corps may have a movement to execute this evening or tomorrow morning'. . . .

I have just returned from the quarters of the 92nd regiment, where I went after we had dined. I found M. de Tocqueville, who is in temporary command of the brigade, bending over a map of the Maine. He informed me that we should have to fight the two armies of Prince Frederick Charles and the Grand Duke of Mecklenburg; that we still formed the left wing of Chanzy's army, and that the 30th regiment would start the day following for La Trugale, a village six kilometers distance from Coulaines, on the high road to Ballon.

La Trugale, Tuesday, 10 January, evening

For some days it had been less cold, and was thawing almost everywhere. Yesterday, just as we were starting, the snow began to fall heavily, and now it lies six inches deep. From constant tramping it has become so slippery that our superior officers can scarcely continue their march on horseback. If we have far to go, as seems likely, it will be a suffering time for us.

We have been in this little hamlet since yesterday morning. Our quarters are very tolerable, and we can get all we want. But we are very sad, for our colonel has left us; he is gone to his post at the extreme positions occupied by the battalion of Saint-Lô, half a league farther on upon the high road. He told us he should return; but what can we reckon upon in times like these? Our new major, M. de Graville de Mailly, has been laid up at Le Mans for some days, very ill with typhoid fever; we are in consequence under the command of Captain Montécot.

Since the morning we have heard the firing of cannon very near. It is undoubtedly becoming serious.

Savigné L'Evêque, Thursday, 12 January, morning

Here we have been since yesterday, entirely separated from our brigade and our regiment. We were coming away at 8 a.m. from General du Temple, who had called us together to give us an address on our duties as officers, when Captain Montécot received orders to start alone with his battalion for Savigné-l'Evêque, and to place himself at the disposal of the general division; it appears that the first brigade, commanded by General Stefani, is threatened, and in want of reinforcements; as always, it is the battalion of Mortain that is sent to the rescue. We have marched two good leagues along roads, encumbered with snow. Savigné-l'Evêque is a large village three leagues from Le Mans, on the way to Bonnétable and Bellesme; in taking that road, we have turned away from the extreme left of the army, and have drawn nearer to the centre.

We piled arms at the entrance of the village, and the men were dismissed for three-quarters of an hour. We set forth—F. de Rougé and I—in search of a morsel of bread; and we found a very small one, in an earthenware plate, with some *rilles*, the traditional dish of the people of Maine. On our return, Captain Montécot gave orders that we should take up our quarters in the houses to the right and left of the road. We made haste to get our men lodged, and it was not till after an hour's wrangling with the occupants, and altercations for wood and straw, that we could think of ourselves. Laloi, our confidential emissary, has arrived with his little cart, and for the last three or four hours we have been cooking, eating, and drinking in this little inn-parlour which Rougé has fixed upon for his quarters. From the threshold can be heard a loud and incessant cannonade, mixed with the rolling of the mitrailleuses, and the sharp, crackling sound of the platoon firing. We can form no idea as to what is passing. There is fighting; but that is all we know. When will it be our turn?

Mézières-Sous-Lavardin, Friday, 13 January, evening

When I wrote the history of our retreat to Le Mans, I thought I should never again see a greater misfortune. I was mistaken. Our youth is destined to witness the most immense, the most overwhelming of disasters. France is sinking from one abyss into another, dragged down by the pitiless hand she has taken as her guide; half our generation is destroyed; we, more unhappy than the rest, are reserved to perish the last, after having beheld everything crumbling away around us. Paris, on which the Prussian shells are now falling, is awaiting the destiny of Babylon and of Jerusalem. And yet, not long ago, the papers were taking pains to inform us that active life was good for Gambetta's constitution, and that he had never been in better health!

We passed the night of the 10th in the suburb of Savigné-l'Évêque. It was nine o'clock a.m. when we received orders to take up our arms and advance to the centre of the village, so as to be within reach, if we were needed. We piled arms in a narrow street; the men were warned to be ready at the first signal, and every one went to look for some house where he might sit down for a moment by the fireside. We had received no rations; some oxen were brought and butchered on the Place de l'Eglise, which was soon transformed into a vast slaughter-house. The cold was so intense that the blood of the animals froze on the ground. The meat was cut up and distributed in haste. The cannon was keeping up an incessant thunder, and the road was black with troops on their way to take up their position on the line.

At last the hour so long looked forward to, seemed to have arrived, the bugle-call sounded through the streets, and ten minutes afterwards we had left behind us the last houses of the town. In spite of the cold, which froze their fingers and covered their muskets with rime, our men had never been so active, for the firing was getting nearer and nearer, and they thought that at last they were going to fight, and be of use to their country. Admiral Jaurés passed down the column, uttering some words which I could not hear distinctly; it was the first time we had seen this sombre countenance. We took it as a good sign that we were so near the general-in-chief, and flattered ourselves we should have the opportunity of distinguishing ourselves under his eyes. When we were a quarter of a league from Savigné-l'Évêque we came to the entrance of a large château, quite deserted, which was assigned to us for our quarters. According to the orders given by General Stefani, we threw up breastworks all along the roof of the buildings, and posted our sharp-shooters behind them; the fourth company occupied the principal outhouse.

This château, of which I am not able to learn the name, is on the edge of the plateau of Savigné. On the two sides our view was shut in by the great fir-trees in the park; before us was a large valley, interspersed with clumps of trees and rows of poplars, which also kept out any distant prospect.

There, to the right and left, the battle was raging. We could see nothing; but as night drew on the firing grew more and more furious, though it did not drown the long hurrahs of the barbarians, of which we heard the distant echoes mingling with the sound of their trumpets. When it bacame quite dark we could see the flash of their guns, and several balls came whizzing through the great courtyard.

We fully expected that it would be an important night, and that the Germans would have a chance in the morning of seeing what effect their savage yells could produce on the hearts of the men of Mortain and Sourdeval. Our hope was vain. At six o'clock an order arrived from the brigade—we were to return to Savigné. With inexpressible vexation we left this house, which we had so uselessly devastated, and drew up on the road.

It was at this instant that the frightful news flew through the ranks like a flash of lightning—Le Mans is evacuated! Le Mans is taken![1] At first the effect was not so terrible, for we none of us believed it; besides, we must be marching to Le Mans, since we were returning by

[1] Le Mans fell on 12 January.

Savigné. When we had passed through this town without stopping we turned to the right and took the same road by which we had come the day before. But this was of no significance; we were no longer wanted here; we were on our way to rejoin our regiment—that was all. Nevertheless, it was rumoured that we were on the way to Ballon, which is much farther northwards than La Trugale. We strained our eyes, my lieutenant and I, to see if we could recognise, by the bushes we passed, the road we had come two days before. At the end of two hours there was no longer any doubt that we had taken another direction, and on our emerging from a by-lane we found ourselves all of a sudden on the high road.

The snow was less deep here than in the lanes, and this was a great relief. But we had still ten kilometres before us, and when we came to the first trench dug across the road for purposes of defence we had to wait for a quarter of an hour till the first part of the column had gone over. We were about 5,000 or 6,000 men. What could be the meaning of this movement towards Mamers or Alençon? We were becoming a prey of the greatest anxiety; and fatigue, cold, and hunger were besides beginning to depress and bow down those men who had marched with such a firm and steady step when they thought they were going to the front. Our halts became more frequent and more interminable; it was impossible to sit down or lean against anything, for if we went near the sides of the road we sank deep in the snow. We thought sorrowfully that the miseries of three weeks ago were beginning again, perhaps worse than before; and for what purpose, if Le Mans was taken?

But was it true? When we entered the town of Souligné-sous-Ballon we were so utterly exhausted that our only thought was to find some place to sleep in. We put off all inquiries till the next day. I had the happiness of catching a glimpse of my colonel at the end of a street, of hearing his voice, and of pressing his hand. He had given us up for lost. Then I ran to secure the houses which had been marked out for my company. A tumultuous crowd was already besieging the doors, effecting an entrance either by persuasion or force; and then, drawing the bolts behind them, they assumed an imperious tone, giving themselves out to be majors or staff officers, and sending off in no very gentle language anyone who tried to get in. Notwithstanding all my efforts, part of my company had to content themselves with the shelter of the church. . . . It was now past midnight.

At 4 a.m. the bugles sounded, and we had to start again. We left the imperial highway and took a broad road to the left, which after many descents and windings comes down into the valley of the Sarthe, and crosses the railway near Montbizot. The traces of defeat were becoming more and more evident; the whole division was there; General de Villeneuve had just passed by with his escort. We again hear of 'turning movements'—a phrase too ominous now to make us smile. It took us about six hours to do less than three leagues, the halts were so long and so frequent. We could not stand still—we had to keep incessantly moving our feet up and down to prevent their getting frozen. I did not know till then that snow was so much worse than mud or ice; it increased our sufferings tenfold.

At noon we crossed the bridge of Montbizot, and, after having passed through the village of Saint-Jean d'Assé, we came out on the high-road, which, leaving Le Mans, diverges from that of Ballon and Mamers, and leads to Alençon. Here the column turned to the left, and, thanks to our happy ignorance of General Chanzy's strategy, we for a moment cherished a feeble hope that we were not definitively retreating. Five hundred yards from Saint-Jean we halted and piled arms. One company was detached to occupy a post of observation, and the others had orders to hold themselves in readiness to rejoin their ranks at a moment's notice. A few cannon shots thundered in the distance, and several guns passed rapidly before our piled arms, as though to place themselves in battery on a small hill which closes the view in the direction of Le Mans.

I went in search of Rougé, that we might clear away some of the snow from a corner, and try to light a few sticks. Our faithful soldiers found some food, which they bought for us. We, in our turn, helped them from our purse; and thus, assisting one another, we succeeded during that hour in regaining a little of our energy. When the bugle-call was heard, I cast a glance over the road.

It descends towards Saint-Jean between two rows of poplars, and then rises abruptly on the other side. It is very broad just here. From the rising ground on which I stood, I could count the immense multitudes that were surging onwards like the waves of the sea. There were at least ten parallel columns all mixed up together. Within the space of a few hundred yards, there must have been at least 5,000 men; they were all moving on towards Beaumont-le-Vicomte, or defiling to the left towards Conlie and Sillé. It was still retreat; of that there was no further doubt. The only question remaining was whether we were going to Laval or to Mayenne. As to what had passed at Le

Mans, I could gather but the vaguest accounts, but the result was only too apparent.

From 2 p.m. to 9, we marched as we had done in the morning, taking twice the necessary time, and fatiguing ourselves much more than if we had gone double the distance. We passed, by moonlight, through the woody and picturesque country to the north of Conlie. A fir-wood brings us to this dreary village, where we found a corner for ourselves after we had provided for our men. Our quarters are detestable, and, whatever miseries may be in store for us tomorrow, we shall have no regrets for Mézières.

Near Sillé-le-Guillaume, Sunday, 15 January, 8 a.m.

Never have we suffered so much. The retreat to Nogent, the retreat into Beauce, were nothing in comparison with this.

Yesterday we were eleven hours on the road, marching scarcely two leagues; we began wading through the snow at 8 a.m. In the middle of the day, the orderly officers announced that our halt would last a certain time. An immense stack of faggots in a neighbouring field disappeared in a very few minutes. With great difficulty we succeeded in getting some of them into a blaze under a hedge. We were able to procure a little bread and a sausage, and our comrades envied us our good fortune. We were just beginning to get a little warmth into us, when we had to start again. We crawled on for another league, which took us two or three hours; then, all of a sudden, when it was getting dark, we had to quicken our pace, and run almost without breathing for a quarter of an hour.

This convulsive race brought us to a new imperial high-road—the third we have come to since we left Savigné l'Evêque; this one leads from Le Mans to Mayenne, through Sillé-le-Guillaume. We had hoped that after so frightful a day we might have found tolerable quarters in the little town of Sillé. But when we were within a league's distance from it, we saw the road in front of us illuminated by a yellow smoky glare, and soon the whole horizon seemed on fire. We knew what it meant; we were to encamp, or rather to bivouac, in those fields, which were a foot deep in snow. As we drew nearer, the light became more and more distinct, and our last hopes vanished. At last came our turn: we piled arms, our muskets sinking deep in the snow.

The promise of rations had been a mere deception: the men had neither meat, nor bread — nor any fuel. Cries of anger and woe were heard in the adjoining fields; we were as near despair as we could be. But there was no doubt as to our duty; it was for us to set an example. I called my brave sergeants, whose unfailing good humour had done so much to keep up the spirits of the others, and we set to work to clear away the snow. The quartermaster, Mullois, went and unfastened one of the immense hurdles which enclose the fields in Maine and Anjou, and dragged it into the camp. After many efforts, we got a few half-dry sticks to blaze, and we were soon seated on the larger pieces of wood around the fire. I had at last found Fernand de Rougé, and he came and sat beside us. Laloi having happily arrived with our provisions, we were delivered from the fear of dying of hunger. Few amongst us could sleep; as to pitching our tents, it was not to be thought of. We passed the night in as much cheerful conversation as we could; it was the only way to avoid being overwhelmed with sadness, for the instant the sound of our voices ceased, we heard on every side the wailing of the weary, and the deep, hollow cough of the innumerable sick, broken every now and then by some wild imprecation of despair. How many of our soldiers will pay for this night with their lives? I dare not ask: I know some who will suffer for it for many a long day to come. The want of food and drink had deprived all of them of the power of rallying. As the light of morning gradually dawned upon this scene of desolation, I thought of the retreat from Moscow.

Evron, Monday, 16 January, evening

When daylight came, we shook off the icy torpor which had kept us motionless, though wide awake, during the last hours of the night, and we heaped up our last pieces of wood on the half-extinguished embers of our hearth. Whilst we were waiting for the summons to start, we began again to warm ourselves, to talk, and to make our coffee. At nine o'clock, Captain Montécot came to tell me that the fourth company was appointed to make a reconnaissance on the road we had passed over the day before. It was almost a relief, for those who had any strength left, to put on their knapsacks and leave this dreadful place. We began to retrace our steps down the great road. The traces of this unhappy army's retreat are lamentable. All along the way we met with stragglers, their faces so ghastly, and their whole appearance so pitiable, that it would have been impossible to reproach them for remaining behind. As far as we went we fell in with them; the Germans must have taken them by hundreds. And they say the 16 and 17 Corps are not nearly in such good marching order as the 21st!

Amongst these melancholy looking spectres who were toiling along in the snow, there were some who were leading by the bridle horses reduced to a state even more miserable than their own. What we had never seen in the two former retreats was the number of dead and dying animals, turned into skeletons, and embedded deep in the ice and snow, whilst they were still breathing. I still see before me, on the left of that road to Sillé, a cow that had fallen into a frozen pool at the bottom of the ravine, and was lying there gazing wistfully up towards the road, waiting for death in that fixed and placid attitude. Our own sufferings leave us little pity to spare, and yet our hearts are wrung by sights like these.

When we were a good quarter of a league from the camp, we turned to the left, and passed through a hilly country studded with shrubberies and orchards. The enemy could not, we knew, be far off, and we advanced with the utmost caution. We doubled back as far as the village of Crissé. As we came near it, the peasants told us that the Germans were entering from the other end. I went forwards, and meeting only with a few disabled stragglers, I began to retrace my way back to the camp, according to my instructions. The firing, however, which had been going on for some time, soon became furious, and on coming near the high road, we saw shells bursting on the spot where we should have to rejoin it. We had, therefore, to take a by-lane, and endeavour to get upon the road farther on. A countryman whom we met on the way acted as our guide. We sank up to our knees in the snow which had drifted between the banks, and which concealed rivulets more or less deep, in which we found ourselves now and then suddenly immersed. The men were exhausted; happily they had had the chance of securing some biscuits from a deserted wagon. We tried in vain to get upon the high road a second time. Shells were falling over it in every direction; one came and burst in the midst of my little troop. Evidently the whole Villeneuve division had retreated to Sillé during our absence, and the only way of rejoining it was by passing on to the town, without exposing ourselves any longer to the risk of being uselessly destroyed. We therefore once more took to the by-ways; the musketry fire was growing sharper every moment, and stray bullets came flying through the bushes. At last we saw a tolerably wide track, which we were assured was the road to Sillé. My heart beat fast with the sense of my responsibility. I called Lieutenant Léonce Josset and Sub-Lieutenant Delafosse; we ascertained our exact position, and after a brief reflection I made my decision. We were just coming out of our deep by-lane on to the high road, when a helmet appeared in sight—a German going towards Sillé, peering about in all directions. My corporal fired, and missed him. He did not wait for a second warning, and retreated towards some of his comrades, who at this moment came in view. I gave orders that they should be fired at from a distance of fifty paces, and they disappeared.

Was I cut off with my little troop? Had the Germans got before us on this road, which was our only hope of safety? Or were the men we had seen their extreme vanguard? Several helmets that we saw immediately afterwards in front of us, upon the ridge of the railway embankment, which is parallel to the road, left us but little hope. A few shots dispersed them. I then gave orders to advance, and we began to march rapidly towards Sillé. On the way I ransacked the farm-houses; all were shut up and deserted. My grave Mullois followed close behind me, with his bayonet forward; ten paces behind marched the troop. We were not long before we found, warming themselves in a house, six of King William's fusiliers, who were certainly no great heroes. At the first sight of us, they began uttering loud inarticulate cries, to give us to understand that they surrendered, and without the faintest resistance they delivered up their loaded muskets, with the bayonet fixed, to Mullois. I spoke German, to reassure them, and told them to pack up their baggage. Then I placed them in the centre, keeping one by my side, that I might interrogate him. He confessed that 200 Prussians were lying in ambush on both sides of the road a little farther on, and that we should very soon fall in with them. It would have been madness to encounter such a force with a hundred men marching exposed. With two or three volleys they would have destroyed us to the last man.

I resolved, therefore, to go across the fields, taking a direction parallel to the road, and keeping up, if necessary, a skirmishing fire to clear the way. I had just found a deep lane, when 200 paces before us I saw the Germans. There was no escape; I gave orders to fire. A few seconds afterwards a shower of bullets whizzed over our heads, but only one man was wounded—in the leg. We returned the fire, and, as we did so, began our flank movement, and in a few moments my whole troop was under the shelter of the banks, which were six feet in height. Four of our prisoners had availed themselves of this interlude by attempting to escape. Mullois shot one close to the muzzle; the others got away. The remaining two, with their muskets and their helmets, were left in our power, and half an hour afterwards we presented them to General du Temple, whom we found in the midst of his marines. We had never expected to return; our retreat over hill and dale had been effected under a constant fire of bullets, that passed a few feet over our heads. 'Vive la mobile!' shouted the marines. 'You have done well, sir,' said the general to me. Never was I so happy as when I heard those simple words. Four of our men, including the one who was wounded, but whom we had been able to carry away, are invalided.

We lost no time in rejoining the battalion, which had been spending the day shivering on the top of a hill, without having seen a single enemy. Captain Montécot having given me leave to take my men wherever I liked, on condition of not going beyond reach of communication, I went to a large farm, where, for the first time for many days, the men found wood, straw, bread, and potatoes in abundance. Whilst Mullois was preparing an onion soup, I settled our accounts with the farmer, and talked with the prisoners. I learnt from them that Prince Frederick Charles was at Le Mans, and that we had to do with the 10 Prussian Corps, under the command of General Voigts-Rhetz; our two prisoners came from Oldenburg, under Colonel Lehmann. I took care that they should be well guarded and kindly treated. Today they have been given up into the hands of the Provost-Marshal.

The three hours passed in that farm have been, for all belonging to the fourth company, the happiest of the campaign. Only I could not refrain from a moment's feeling of sadness as I looked upon those brave faces, so weather-beaten, so attenuated, and thought what a poor use had been made of so much courage and fortitude by those who are answerable before God and man for the blood of our armies and the destiny of this nation. . . . At dusk, we had again to resume the scarcely interrupted chain of our tribulations; but our hearts were light, and we marched gaily along, listening with delight to the great drops which were falling from the poplars by the roadside, announcing that the frost was over. We passed through Sillé without stopping; then we left the imperial road leading to Mayenne to take the high road to Evron. An attempt was made to find quarters in a hideous village called Rouessé-Vassé. There was not a quarter of the room we required, and that night was almost as bad as the one before. At four o'clock in the morning the colonel's quarters, in which I had found refuge, caught fire. A franc-tireur was accused of having let fall a lighted match upon the straw. The franc-tireurs have to bear the blame of everything. Whatever may have been the cause, we had to rush headlong downstairs, after groping about in haste for our equipments, and making superhuman efforts to get into our boots, which had shrunk with the wet. The Place de l'Église, in which this house was situated, presented a scene of the most alarming crowd and confusion. Whilst the Mobiles were handing the buckets, the women of the village came and stood round in groups, screaming at the top of their voices. The horses belonging to some Chasseurs d'Afrique who were picketed on the Place, were prancing and striking out in every direction, kicking furiously every time that the great masses of snow, which came sliding down from the roof of the church, fell upon their backs. All this went on in an ocean of icy mud, and ended at length in the extinction of the fire. Soon afterwards the day began to dawn through the fog, and we had to take our departure.

It had been less cold since morning. The roads are in a dreadful state, but our sufferings are mitigated. In many places the snow has disappeared from off the heaps of stones by the wayside; the men can lay their knapsacks on them, and sit down during the moments they are halting. Also, we have been marching in less fatiguing order. We had a long halt in the middle of the day, and, after a stretch of four leagues, we arrived by daylight at this pretty little town of Évron.

General du Temple was resolved to make amends to us for the two bad nights we have passed, and he has succeeded. We have never been so comfortable even at Coulaines, and we could wish for nothing better than to stay here. But we must not think of it. 'Tomorrow, 17 January at five a.m., the second battalion of the 30th regiment will muster in front of its quarters, and then will be supplied with fresh meat as it passes through the market.' . . .

Commune de Contest, near Mayenne, Wednesday, 18 January

This terrible retreat is drawing to a close; we shall no doubt be drawn up here for some time in these small cottages, scattered like so many islands in a sea of mud.

Yesterday we marched seven leagues; the weather was fine; the muddy roads were glazed and slippery. We had breakfast at Jublains. Since we left Évron we have been out of reach of the Germans. We find a country less desolated, the peasants less alarmed, and a few shops open in the villages; we can even get bread, if we take pains to seek for it. The landscape is gradually throwing off her melancholy mantle of snow, which has for so many days deprived us of all the consolations of nature. The picturesque hills of the Maine are by degrees showing their heads again, and we begin once more to look about us. Since our departure from Le Mans misery has prevented us from raising our eyes from the ground.

When we entered Mayenne it was black night. We marched right through the town, which is a very long one; and, on reaching the farthest end, we had to remain standing for an hour under arms, before any quarters were assigned to us. We had been on our feet since 5 a.m., and we were sinking from fatigue. At last a few houses were marked out for us, in which we disposed of the seven hundred men remaining of the battalion as well as we could. This morning we have done two leagues on the road to Laval, and we are now quartered at Grand-Launay, a cluster of two or three farm-houses at twenty minutes' distance from Contest. We have not had time as yet to explore the neighbourhood, and we are enjoying the luxury of such rest as can be obtained in these dismal dens, whose unfortunate owners are left without knowing where to lay their heads.

Le Grand-Launay, Sunday, 29 January

We are leading here a monotonous and secluded existence—one day is like another; if it does not snow it rains; this is the only variety presented to us. For the last few days we have had drill four hours a day; the rest of the time we stagnate in our farm-houses. We make no excursions for the passage of the troops and the thaw together have broken up all the roads, which makes a drive in a cart not a very agreeable pastime. The peasants are a good and obliging sort of people; it makes one feel all the more for them in the heavy burden imposed upon them by our presence. Their fields are trodden down, their fuel is consumed, their straw carried off. It is true that we never fail to give them orders on the commissariat stores, but that does not indemnify them for a quarter of what they lose. In the cottage in which

I am quartered, the poor woman of the house does not dare, in spite of all my entreaties, to come near the fire. She spends her days shivering and weeping in a dark corner. The cattle disease is making havoc in her stable—her oxen are dying one after the other. Her husband has lost an arm, and her sons are little children. The sight of this family fills one with sorrow.

On the 24th, General du Temple passed us in review. He had the opportunity of ascertaining that the most numerous of our companies consisted only of 100 men; at Coulaines the average was still 120. What must be left, then, of those companies which have been seriously engaged?

Our colonel is quartered more than a quarter of a league away, with the Saint-Lô battalion, and it is a serious undertaking to pay him a visit. Now and then he comes and dines with us, as in the good old days that are gone, and for one evening we are happy. All the battalions of the brigade are echeloned on the by-lane to Laval, which joins the great imperial road farther on; we are those who are nearest to Contest, which is the seat of the division. General du Temple is with his marines at a league's distance, at Laval, at the château of Montgiroux.

We think with fond regret of our quarters at Coulaines and our dinners at Le Mans. Mesdames de Grainville and de Rougé cannot come to these muddy solitudes. M. de Rougé has passed twenty-four hours with us, and has made us feel that we have heard some echoes from our dear Norman country.

It is very seldom we get any information from the newspapers. We still have but a very vague idea of all that has been passing lately. The forces of Brittany, which were united under the command of Jaurès, have just been detached from the 21 Corps to go to the defence of their province. M. de Charette, who was in command of the volunteers from the west, has been appointed general. Major de Couëssin has received the cross of the Legion d'Honneur for the gallant resistance he made at Yvré-l'Evêque, after the heights of Montfort-le-Rotrou were abandoned. In an official letter today, General Chanzy takes leave of the Zouaves in the most flattering terms.

What is to be our fate? No one has the least idea. As no mention is made either of peace or of a truce, we must have gained some successes in the other parts of France, or at all events our armies elsewhere must still be in tolerable condition. Since the battle of Bapaume we know nothing of the north, and no news of Bourbaki's army has reached us. Here the disaster has been complete—the 16th and 17th corps have been entirely routed—nothing is left of them but a mere wreck. Our losses in the battle of Le Mans, were it is said, considerable; but the retreat is reckoned to have cost us 27,000 men. If we are still resolved on war to the last extremity, we must make up our minds to carry it on in a very different manner. If the Germans were to enter La Manche and Brittany they would find, I suspect, a reception very different from that which they met with in Beauce. But for the present they are a great distance off, and we hear scarcely anything of them. It is certain another battle is in contemplation, for in an order lately read out, the troops were given to understand they were to dismiss all thoughts of retreat. Nothing but their respect for authority prevents the men from returning this hint to their generals. Our brave Du Temple, however, does not deserve it, and I do not think it was General de Villeneuve who lost the battle of Le Mans.

We certainly must have contracted an invincible love of retreat and turning movements if we were to give up to the enemy the splendid positions we are now occupying. Some days ago, being on outpost duty with my company, I had to leave this world of hedges and muddy fields in which our existence just now is spent, to go and spend the night on the banks of the Mayenne. The deep lanes, which might be called ravines at the best of times, are now perfect quagmires, so that we march across the fields; an imperceptible ascent brings us at the end of ten minutes on to a high table-land. . . . Sixty feet below us flows the broad and rapid Mayenne; its course for a long way is nearly parallel with the Laval road and the line of our cantonments. The right bank is almost the whole way along exceedingly precipitous; an assault would be impossible; nevertheless, to make sure of not being surprised, we line the borders of these precipices every night with sentries. You get down to the river by clinging to the rocks, the trees, and the brambles. The great moss-covered stones, the impetuous torrent, and the buzzards soaring in wide circles over the chasm, give a wild and rural aspect to the valley, though the effect is a little spoilt by some large new mills which have been built at intervals along it. The water, imprisoned by the mill dams, curls itself into a sheet of foam, and makes the whole place resound with a mournful and ceaseless echo. This view has no celebrity, but it is worthy of an artist's hand. When we get weary of gazing upon it, we return to the hospitable hearth of M. Leroux, a wealthy farmer, in whose house the companies on outpost duty are quartered. Near this house stands a ruin, which, he says, dates as far back as the days of the English.

There is every indication of that ancient chimney and those indestructible walls having belonged to the fifteenth century. His own dwelling is like all the Norman farms, which are built in so curious and picturesque a style. Signs of rustic opulence are visible in the long massive table with its two traditional seats, the shining cupboards, the sideboard adorned with crockery, and above all the immense fireplace, overhung with the monumental mantelpiece, supported by two huge brackets of stone.

It is a march of five miles up the river from Leroux's farm to Mayenne. I went there the day before yesterday. There is nothing fine or interesting about the town. The river divides it in half. The bridges are ready to be blown up on the approach of the enemy. The streets are all pretty nearly a match for one another in ugliness. A taste for the olden time finds nothing more there to gratify it than a love for the new and showy. We saw nothing there of the ancient gables which add distinction to provincial towns; and I looked in vain, not for a sanctuary where mass is said, but for the parish or collegiate church, the old Gothic edifice of our fathers. They have run up a new one in modern lancet style. On the right bank I saw the ruins of a fortress, whose ramparts appear to be turned into a public promenade. I had not time to explore them.

Le Grand-Launay, Friday, 3 February

Our situation is unchanged; rain and mud are still our element. This morning, by the general's order, we had to march a league to go and manoeuvre in the park of the Château de Marie, on the Laval road; we came back drenched. These duties are not favourable to the men's health; the number of sick is increasing, and it is in vain that our kind Dr Hautraye (from Saint-Hilaire) bestows all his care and attention upon them. M. Guérin, a very skilful chemist from the same part of the country, emulates the devotion of M. Hautraye, and shares his fatigues; their ambulance is well supplied, and is of the greatest service to us. Our excellent friend M. Bidard, who has been with us from the beginning of the campaign, is left at Sillé, seriously ill.

Our minds are as much agitated as our limbs are benumbed, and whilst the earth and sky are both of the same dull, leaden hue, the political horizon is as black as night.

Paris has surrendered, an armistice is signed, and the war apparently is at an end. Elections for a National Assembly are coming on. The armistice is to last twenty days. On the evening of 30 January, an order was received from General Jaurès for the suspension of all hostilities. But the greatest precautions are still recommended, and we continue to keep watch on the banks of the Mayenne.

In these days of egotism and apathy, the first idea one has is always of a personal kind, and political questions are regarded in relation to one's own private convenience; consequently our first thought on receiving this intelligence was that we should now be able to get leave of absence, and see our friends again. It has been a general weakness with all of us, and I must confess that I was one of the first to share it; after all we have suffered, it will not perhaps be thought inexcusable. But now that I reflect upon it, I cannot blame General Jaurès for having refused to allow any of us to absent ourselves. . . .

General du Temple and Colonel de Tocqueville, who are offering themselves for election in the Department of La Manche, have declared for a free Assembly. The way in which they refrain from pronouncing definitively for peace or for war is in very good taste. One is merely left to feel, under their impassioned and forcible language, that they are ready for any sacrifices. But they boldly demand of those who are arbitrarily gambling away our blood and our fortunes to give account of their conduct of affairs, and to say whether they pretend to be leading us. The circular of the young major of the 92nd regiment is quite a judicial address; that of General du Temple presents us with a brief and energetic declaration of principles. M. de Sainte-Marie, another volunteer who has given up a most enviable position to serve his country, offers himself to our suffrages, and gives us a programme as well considered as it is well expressed.

These documents were read the day before yesterday at the mess tables of Saint-Lô, and secured an almost unanimous support to the ideas which they enunciated. I had on that very day to wait upon General du Temple, and there I went with my Colonel as soon as we rose from table. The General was gracious, dignified, serious; he apprised us of his intention to come forward, which we did not yet know officially, and explained to us in a few words his ideas on the position of affairs. When I took leave of him, he was pleased to tell me that he had believed me lost on 15 January, together with my company; and that he was asking on my behalf for the honorary recognition of my services.

Yesterday I went to Mayenne, in the hope of finding some news in the papers. I could not ascertain what had become of Bourbaki's and Faidherbe's armies. If they are still in existence, no one can say what resolution the Assembly we are about to elect may not be capable of; but this silence on the part of the Government and newspapers is the silence of the grave. . . .

Friday, 10 February

General Félix du Temple set out some days ago on his electioneering tour, and has left Colonel de Grainville in command of the brigade.

On the 6th I went to Mayenne. There I read the history of our disasters. Faidherbe, after a desperate struggle, has been overpowered by numbers near Saint-Quentin. Bourbaki has attempted to commit suicide. His army has endured the last extremity of misery, and has had to pass over into Switzerland, where it has been disarmed and interned.

The elections took place on the 8th. . . .

The rain and the mud together kept many of the country-people away. As to our Gardes Mobiles, they appeared fully to comprehend the importance of the public duty they were called upon to fulfil; the battalion of Mortain marched to the poll with praiseworthy calmness and dignity. I gazed on that long line of brave men, reduced by war and misery to less than half their number; but I thought to myself that, after all, the sufferings they had gone through would not have been quite fruitless—many of those young men, once so turbulent, are now tried and serious men, whose words and whose example will have in their own neighbourhood the most beneficial influence.

Our daily life continues unaltered; our view never changes—the earth and sky are still grey and dreary; our thoughts are black. All leave of absence is refused more rigorously than ever.

This morning we hear a rumour that we are to be sent to the south. We shall go where we are ordered. But if it is to carry on the war, the defiles of our Norman Switzerland will be given up to the enemy without our having the power of defending them. After having lost half their number in the service of their common country, the men of Mortain have some right to be allowed to protect their own hearths.

Andouillé, Between Mayenne and Laval, Sunday, 12 February, 5 p.m.

We are on our way to the south; some say we are to stop at Niort or Poitiers, others that we are to go on to Bordeaux; no one really knows. The order for our departure came yesterday afternoon, and we started this morning at ten. We look back with no regret upon our miserable quarters, nor upon that land of mud where we had not two days' fine weather; nor upon those broken-up roads, where we were nearly upset at every step, when we made a pilgrimage to Mayenne in such vehicles as we could procure, drawn by an animal more or less apocalyptic.

A few rays of sunlight cheered us in the early part of our march, but after we left Montgiroux the rain began to fall in torrents. It is only since the last hour that we have found shelter from the deluge which is pouring down harder than ever. The road we have passed over is not very interesting. No fine views, except a few glimpses of the Mayenne valley, near M. de Robien's château. Andouillé is a large commonplace village, with a new church and a number of cafés. The whole division marches together. The arrangements for our quarters are made in defiance of all common sense. If the same system is pursued to the end, this march in time of peace will be like one of our most memorable retreats, which is saying a great deal. The consequences must be the same; armies so conducted melt away before one's eyes. . . . Chanzy's troops are now reduced to 31,000 men, of which 10,000 only belong to the 16th and 17th Corps.

L'Huisserie, near Laval, Tuesday, 14 February, morning

Marching in file has become once more our daily occupation, and will continue to be so, no doubt, for some time to come.

Unfortunately, our men are miserably shod; and we have fallen back into the habit of starting very late to do five or six leagues, so that we do not reach our quarters till night has set in. Yesterday, as the day before, there was room only for 200 out of 600 men. F. de Rougé had to make a long excursion over the fields in search of some farm, which he succeeded at last in finding.

The mud is still deep, but the weather has become very mild; for the first time for a long while we have been reminded what it is to

feel warm, and we took off our cloaks on the march. This memorable
event took place as we were approaching Laval by the banks of the
Mayenne; the view of this town, coming to it from the north, is lovely.
The river runs on the left amongst the poplars, as broad almost as the
Seine. On the right the road is overhung by beautiful rocks, of a warm
tint, intermingled with brambles, and glowing golden in the rays of
the sun. On leaving the fine quays of Laval, the same kind of landscape
reappears, and continues for some way, but the colouring is different;
the hill casts over the road and river broad black shadows. On the
opposite bank the slope spreads itself in green swards, which must be
beautiful in summer; mills, with small hamlets, are scattered along
the shore. Our fatigue and the prosaic business of finding quarters
render us almost insensible to the beauties of nature; our one thought
when we see a cottage is, how many Mobiles it can be made to hold—
quite a new point of view for the tourist. For the last league the heaps
of stones by the roadside were covered with stragglers.

Château-Gontier, Wednesday, 15 February, 10 a.m.

Yesterday's march was long and wearisome; heat had made its
appearance the day before, and thirst came with it. A month ago our
one desire when we halted was to get a few sticks to light—now what
we crave for is cider. As we get nearer to the south, the country people
are less obliging, and the farmers' wives are perfect harpies.

We were far away from that cool valley which we skirted for a
whole day so delightfully; instead of the romantic promontory of
Saint-Jean-sur-Mayenne, we have had for remarkable objects a coal
mine and a few slate quarries. After an eight hours' march we arrived
—as usual, at night—at Château-Gontier.

To find shelter for my men, I had to force open the door of a very
elegant house, which had, unhappily for the owners, been left entirely
deserted. A certain amount of damage was inevitable, and the beautiful
gilt furniture was injured. The young couple who had prepared this
pretty dwelling for themselves had forgotten to leave anyone in
charge of it. This morning their agent came to the house where I had
taken refuge, at some distance from my troops, to make his complaints.
I was listening with resignation, when all at once I discovered, to my
great confusion, that they were cousins to the excellent lady who had

received my lieutenants and myself with such true hospitality. . . .
Such is war! . . .

This morning, at eleven, we start for Lion d'Angers.

Avirré, Thursday, 16 February, morning

It is not at Lion d'Angers, as we were told, but in this little
village, a good league from the high road, that we have taken up our
quarters, after a day of heavy rain. This time it was I who had to go
in search of lodgings, the administrative powers taking it for granted
that men can be piled up in a house like figs in a box. I found a farm-
house of the true Norman type—no doubt the last we shall see in this
journey of the tropics; endless cupboards, beds as high as one's head,
to get out of which one must put one's feet together and drop straight
down, either into one's boots or on to the muddy floor. All these
houses are fitted up in the same style.

Brissac, Saturday, 18 February

For the first time since the days of Le Mans, I have been spending the night under the roof of a friend. It is twelve years since I was
here, but I had an accurate recollection of this magnificent dwelling.
Today it is almost empty; there is missing that poetic figure of the
lady of the house, with her powdered hair, and her ever youthful
smile, which can never be forgotten by those who have once seen it.
There are missing the Duc de Brissac and his three sons. Maurice was
in the dragoons; he is now languishing at Deissenfels, in Saxony, a
victim, like so many others, to the incapacity or the treachery of
Bazaine. Roland, though he had passed the legal age, has joined the
Mobiles; he is at Besançon. Pierre has for some time been with his
father, who is marching with the Army of the Loire, at the head of an
ambulance he has established. The young marquise is alone at the
castle, and does the honours with much grace.

I dined here with General Guyon, who was in command of our
division when we were in Beauce. He is now at the head of all the
cavalry of the 21 Corps, which still numbers two thousand, but not
one regiment, and scarcely one complete squadron. Amongst the
general's staff there is a tall American officer holding the rank of major,

and who is taken by many people for the Duc de Chartres, though he has not the slightest resemblance to him. This supposed Prince of Orleans is nothing but a fine and brave volunteer, such as America ought to reckon in greater numbers, when it is a question of defending the country of Lafayette and of Rochambeau.

I have been spending the morning wandering round these venerable walls, for which I feel as great an admiration as does my faithful servant Richard. But we must bid them farewell, for the hope of a delay at Angers was but a deception. We are to march today as yesterday, and they say we shall not rest till we reach Poitiers.

From Membrolle, after a tolerable night, we pursued our way to Angers, which we passed through in file before Admiral Jaurès. The battalion was quartered in the village of Saint-James, where we heard that we were to start again the next day. Today the column is passing under these windows on its way towards Loudun. The second brigade will soon be here; let us go where duty calls us.

La Châlérie, Sunday, 19 February, morning

This hamlet, where we have just been spending the night, is only two leagues from Brissac, and some 100 yards on the left of the high road leading to Loudun. Our quarters were pretty good, thanks to our new Adjutant-Major Breillot, who takes the greatest pains and fulfils his duties conscientiously.

The windmills, the flat roofs, the stunted vines, and cisterns of Anjou, with their long wooden poles, have succeeded to the hedges, the fences, and the pointed gables of the Maine. We can get no more cider, and our men have recourse (sometimes at the expense of our straight line) to the thin alcoholic wine, which gives the people of Anjou all the wit they have. The Loire is very full just now, though not to overflowing, and the celebrated view of Ponts-de-Cé was exquisitely beautiful. If the Germans should cross the river, these fair vineyards will be burned and the district ruined for a long time to come.

These farms beyond the Loire are dull and ugly. The women who inhabit them have sometimes rather pretty faces under their eccentric headgears; but the little girls who are adorned with this singular roofing look like perfect monkeys. The men are sulky and obtuse.

129

Trois-Moustiers, Wednesday, 22 February

There is no beauty in this part of France. Montreuil-Bellay is an oasis in the midst of a desert where one nearly dies of thirst. . . .

The road to the Trois-Moustiers was very uninteresting. We were warned that we should find bad quarters there, and so we did; but no imagination can conceive a more barbarous locality in a civilised region than Moustier. It is half a league distant from the high road. The principal street is a deep lane, and the doors of the houses look like entrances to cellars. The inhabitants are brutish and idiotic, and hide away everything they have; they cannot be induced even to give us anything for money. Their supreme dread seems to be lest they should have to part with anything they possess. . . .

Another miserable night; . . . but we cannot be very far from the villages General Guyon spoke of, when I dined with him at Brissac, as being the end of our journey.

Angliers, Thursday, 23 February

At last here we are for some days in comfortable quarters. We were to have encamped on the heights of Mirebeau, a large town farther on towards Poitiers, and a terrible picture was drawn of the hard life we should lead there. But this morning, just as we were starting, a counter-order arrived, and we are to remain at Angliers. Our friends have dispersed on exploring expeditions into the neighbourhood. I am here alone in my farm-house, with Fernand de Rougé, who has been ill of fever for the last three days, and is still very feeble.

No doubt we are glad to have left the mud and the cold of the north; but when the leaves come out we shall regret our dear green Normandy. Notwithstanding the hope of our approaching disbandment, which is beginning to stir our hearts, I keep repeating to my friends that we must expect to be under arms for some time yet to come; for Chanzy's army is now the only existing force, and so long as our imprisoned troops are not returned and reorganised, it would be madness, in the face of all the civil troubles with which the country is threatened, to dismiss the last soldiers who are still capable of marching. No doubt we are an expensive body, but there are some economies worse than any extravagances.

VI

Aftermath

The dangers which Roger de Mauni foresaw as an aftermath of the war, against which he wished to see some disciplined forces retained, were not slow to declare themselves. But first there was the question of the peace. The size of the financial indemnity was not unexpected, but the territorial demands were harsh; much harsher than Bismarck knew to be wise and an indication of how far the war faction, including von Moltke and the German people, had descended into bitterness. It was expected that the Germans would demand Alsace with Strasbourg, but it was hoped to save Lorraine and Metz for France. Bismarck himself was very reluctant to acquire this piece of purely French territory, but von Moltke was adamant in his view that its acquisition was essential for strategic reasons. As a result, one-fifth of Lorraine, which included Metz, together with the whole of Alsace was ceded to Germany. On one point only did Bismarck give way, and that was over Belfort. The heroic resistance of the garrison, which had marched out with the honours of war on 17 February, had made the city very dear to the French. As it was unlikely to have any strategic significance, Bismarck agreed to except it from the rest of Alsace, but in return he demanded the right of the German army to make a triumphal entry into Paris, an event which had been specifically excluded by the terms of the armistice. In consequence, the German troops entered Paris on 1 March, but, thanks to the speed with which the Assembly ratified the treaty, spent only forty-eight hours within the city. As they left, the Parisians lit bonfires in the streets to 'purify' them after the German presence.

Yet there was a far greater trial in store for the unfortunate city. On 18 March, there was popular resistance when the authorities attempted to recover from the heights of Montmartre a number of National Guard cannons. Almost in spite of themselves the leaders of the Left found themselves as revolutionaries in possession of the city, Thiers and the legal government having withdrawn immediately to Versailles. For two months the legal government (popularly known as the Versaillais) built up their forces as the revolutionary Left (the Communards) organised its control of Paris and continued to defy them. Bismarck offered the use of German troops to dislodge the insurgents, for the Army of Occupation remained on the eastern perimeter of Paris. Not unnaturally, Thiers refused, but obtained instead permission to increase the agreed size of the French regular army and to speed up the return of the prisoners. By May an army of 130,000 had been assembled. Ducrot and Trochu had disappeared from high command—the new leader was Marshal MacMahon, prisoner of war since the day he had fallen wounded at Sedan. On the 21st of the month his army broke into Paris and for a week—*la semaine rouge de mai*—drove the insurgents back through the barricaded streets lit by the flames of the great public buildings fired by the Communards in an orgy of destruction. By 28 May, it was all over, save for the executions. The revenge was frightful and far exceeded the atrocities committed by the Commune. In the same month Jules Favre and Bismarck signed the Treaty of Frankfurt, the definitive treaty of the Franco-Prussian War.

All this was a long way from the Battalion of Mortain. On 1 March they still formed part of Chanzy's Army, though by now they were beginning to wonder what the future had in store for them.

Angliers, Wednesday, 1 March

We are taking root in this dismal place. Our life is not hard—only monotonous. Now that the order has been given for us to resume our daily drill, our limbs are in exercise morning and evening, but our minds remain inactive; we have very few newspapers or books. Politics are in a chaos, and the war has no longer any future that we can look forward to; since the prolongation of the armistice, a renewal of hostilities has become so improbable that we think of nothing now but of our disbandment and our return home. Our colonel is acting as general; he is quartered a long way off, and we seldom get a sight of him. We are vegetating in dullness and torpor.

Thursday, 2 March

Peace is signed—the papers tell us at what price. . . .

Angliers, Sunday, 5 March, morning

Last night came an order for a grand review by the general of division. We started early, and were two leagues on our way when the news arrived that the review was countermanded, and that we were to make our way to Jaulnay, a station on the Bordeaux line, three leagues from Poitiers. Tomorrow, it appears, or the day after we are to take the railroad for some unknown destination, which may perhaps be Bordeaux, or more likely Paris, or, more likely still, Cherbourg, or Saint-Lô; in this last case, it would be the end. It is high time; our men are falling ill one after the other—the inevitable consequence of all that they have had to suffer.

Saint-Georges, near Poitiers, 6 March, Monday

Forty-eight hours more of misery. The day before yesterday, including the useless morning's march, we went twelve leagues. On reaching the village of Chêneché, which was assigned to us for quarters, we found it already occupied. It was black night; our poor fellows had nothing to eat or drink, and nowhere to sleep; many of them could no longer stand; this climate is not made for them. With great efforts I succeeded in housing thirty of my men who could still crawl; the rest remained lying in the dust, as did a good many of the officers also. I tried in vain to drag Christian de Failly with me in search of a house; he was incapable of another step. . . .

Never did our sufferings seem harder to bear than now, when we have no hope or even desire left to sustain us.

Today we made only three or four leagues, but they appeared very long for we had been told it would only be six kilometres. Truth is set aside in little things as in great—nothing is more exasperating.

We arrived early at this village, which looks gay and smiling; we found good quarters. Saint-Georges lies hidden in one of the many undulations of the ground on the right bank of the Clain. . . .

. . . Our effectives are reduced in number by more than sixty since we left the banks of the Mayenne.

Saint-Georges, Wednesday, 8 March

Nothing of any interest in the papers—nothing new as to our

destination. Nevertheless the spring is drawing near; the cherry trees
are in full blossom, and the peasants are pruning their vines. When
we look again on the cascades at Mortain, the snow will have long
since disappeared, and the wind will be murmuring amongst the
leaves.

Friday, 10 March

When will the last day come? Despondency is creeping over us;
it is time for all this to be at an end. Where are those days when the
end was still an uncertainty, and when hope, faint though it was, gave
us wings? This life without thought, this inactivity without repose, is
killing us. Fernand de Rougé is ailing; Viallet is very ill; Christian de
Failly has gone to rejoin the depot at Cherbourg—every day brings
some new cause for sadness. Happily our colonel is here; he dines at
our mess as in former times, and sets us all an example of good
humour.

We have now hardly any drill. Our leisure hours are spent in
listening to all sorts of contradictory rumours as to our disbandment.
Two days ago it was said we were to march to Saint-Lô; today the
idea is denounced as an absurdity. . . .

The optimists are of opinion that we shall be sent home by the railroad; we are only waiting, they say, till the lines are less obstructed. . . .

Sunday, 12 March

The end of our troubles is at hand. Here is the order just brought
from headquarters—

'According to the instructions contained in the circular of 9 March
the General Commander-in-Chief of the 21 Corps d'armée will give
up his command to General de Villeneuve, of the third division of
infantry.

'This general officer will proceed to disband the troops. He will be
assisted in this operation by General Rousseau, in command of the
first division, and by General Guyon, who is at the head of the cavalry.
. . . General Stefani, in command of the first brigade, will take the
command of the third division.'

The dissolution of Chanzy's army began some time ago, and is going on visibly every day. The soldiers of the line who have served their time are already sent back to their homes; two or three of them were in our battalion as military instructors. Yesterday, long strings of artillery wagons were going towards Chaseneuil. I imagine that the 16th and the 17th Corps have ceased to exist. A little patience, and our turn will come.

Thursday, 16 March

Only one thing more was wanting to fill the measure of our vexation; it was that we should be sent home disarmed, like a troop of beggars. Such is the decision of the Minister of War. In the letter in which he gives this order he expresses his regret, alleging as his reason that our muskets are absolutely necessary for the troops now being organised at Versailles to keep the Parisians in order. It seems to me, however, that some pains might have been taken to avoid offering such an affront to soldiers who have always made a good use of the arms now to be taken from them. Why not have demanded those which are detained in Switzerland? They would be given, now that peace is signed. But the Garde Mobile is no longer wanted, and is treated accordingly. . . . Our lot is to return humbly to our provinces, and to be forgotten. Rewards were spoken of some little while ago. I imagine that no one would look for anything of that sort after such disasters. But I do not think that we are showing undue self-esteem in expecting to be sent back to Mortain as soldiers, rather than as vagrants. We have never been vainglorious, and the slaughter at Thiron is nothing by the side of 1,000 imaginary battles, but we will never allow ourselves to be despised.

If the question were one of personal satisfaction, one would have no hesitation in setting an example of self-abnegation; but the effect produced by this resolution can only be disastrous. All military spirit will be for ever destroyed amongst those men who have seen nothing but the evils of war, and who have been made to bear its dishonours when they have not deserved it. How can they ever retain any good associations with the profession of arms, after they have been treated like this? Yet, if France is to remain a nation, it is evident that the second echelon of her forces ought to be considered worthy of respect. . . . Nothing has been learnt, and it would seem as if everything had been forgotten.

The joy of seeing the end of their sufferings approaching prevents the men from feeling too acutely the affront that has been offered them. They are doing their best to furbish up their guns, so as to restore them in respectable condition, and they are quietly making ready for the longest journey we have yet had to undertake. We are to return to La Manche on foot; the distance is from sixty to seventy leagues, and will be divided into twelve day's marches.

General Stefani's order, dated 15 March, says that 'the five battalions of La Manche are to give up their arms, equipments, and articles of encampment at Poitiers, on 18 March, and to start on the 19th. These battalions will be quartered on the 18th in the Faubourg de Porteau'. We are told that our marches will be less laborious and our quarters better than on former occasions, but we have been too often deceived to place the least confidence in any promises. Generals Chanzy and Jaurès have in their last orders taken leave of us in very flattering terms. They bear witness that we have done our duty, and bestow great praise upon us, which I believe many of the soldiers in this battalion well deserve. But what importance can be attached to words which are repeated indiscriminately by everybody to everybody? I am weary of this universal praise giving. If everyone in France has deserved nothing but compliments, whom shall we accuse of our disasters? Can we believe that we have not been guilty of a series of grave errors? Is it right that we should all be praising one another, when the work we have accomplished is before our eyes? Where are the guilty? Where are the incapable, the weak, the self-seeking? For such there must be—above, below, and everywhere—to account for such results as we have seen. Who will tell us the truth? Let us accept these official words with due respect, and let us be grateful for the goodwill of those who send them, and who have, no doubt, like ourselves, done their best. But let us none the less examine our conscience; let us confess that this nation, which worships itself even in the hour of humiliation, is not what it ought to be, and needs to be regenerated from its roots.

The reading of these two documents made little impression on the troops, and, with all the gratitude we owe to our generals, I do not see how it could be otherwise. General du Temple's, and still more our colonel's farewells, went more to our hearts. The general's was as follows:

'Officers and soldiers of the second brigade!—I seem to have left you for some time to fulfil important and anxious duties in the National Assembly, but I have not been absent from you in thought.

I have not seen you enduring cold and hunger, marching day and night through snow and mud, and facing the enemy's fire, if not like old soldiers, yet like brave Frenchmen, without often admiring—and always loving you. I have striven to set you an example. I went before when we marched towards the enemy, and behind you when we retreated. I often rose the first, and never lay down to rest till I had sought some shelter for you. Remember me, that you may do the same; think of me not only as your general, who is proud of having commanded you, who congratulates you upon your obedience, but also as one who will be always ready to help you when he can, and who will never forget the brave marines, and the brave sons of La Manche and Calvados, whom he has had the honour of commanding.

> 'The General commanding the
> 'Second brigade,
> (Signed) 'DU TEMPLE.'

'Officers and Gardes Mobiles!—The generals who have been at your head through this severe and suffering campaign, have all in turn addressed you their farewells, and bestowed upon you the praise you so well deserve. I can add nothing to their words; but, happier than they, I return with you to your homes to live in the midst of you. Remember me with kindness, and let me feel that you are my friends. My own affection has long been given to you. Never shall I forget the honour of having commanded you.

> 'Colonel of the 30th regiment.
> (Signed) 'DE GRAINVILLE.'

Poitiers, Faubourg de Porteau, Sunday, 19 March, morning

The 30th regiment is to take the high road to Loudun, whilst the 92nd goes by Thouars. We shall thus not be more than 2,000 men together, which will greatly lighten our fatigue.

I thought that yesterday would never come to an end. We left Saint-Georges in good order at 8 a.m., carrying for the last time those arms which we received four months ago with so much eagerness, and which, happily, have not been altogether useless. The column slowly traversed the whole length of the town of Poitiers, to go and deposit their muskets at the Lyceum. The ceremony was long and sad. My heart was full when for the last time I gave the order to my ninety brave soldiers to put their bayonets on their muskets, and to pile arms. The *chassepots* were given up first, with their cases; then the cartridges were poured out in a heap and carried away. We had also to restore our tents, rugs, camp-kettles, and saucepans. Finally, each man took off his belt and cartridge box, and we left that courtyard—in which the whole equipment of the regiment, piled up in irregular heaps, presented the appearance of a vast scene of pillage. I never thought that those poor chattels could have been so dear to me. The men are happy. Poor fellows! they have a right to be so, and I should be sorry to damp their joy with the bitter thoughts that oppress me.

We had a league to march before we reached our quarters. This Faubourg de Porteau is on the other side of the Clain, opposite the road by which we entered Poitiers. From the top of the cliffs there is a beautiful view over the river and the town. Five hundred yards off is the great high road to Mirebeau, which we are about to follow.

Scarcely had we given up our muskets, than we began to experience the annoyances which are sure to beset a troop of disarmed soldiers. The townspeople looked insolent, and hardly moved on one side to let us pass; I was in a state of concentrated rage. I ordered one man, who refused to get out of our way, to be seized, and I made him march the rest of the way with us as a criminal; then, after giving him a good fright, I dismissed him with contempt. At the Faubourg de Porteau the people closed their doors against us, declaring that their houses and their beds were not made for the Mobiles. Two of them were about to assault me; I took my pistol and threatened to blow their brains out, well knowing that there would be no necessity for such extreme measures.

The rugs and the camp equipages which our men have had to give up are sadly missed; unless their quarters are carefully seen to, they will suffer more than ever. The nights are still very cold, and after marching the whole day in the hot sun, they have nothing to cover themselves with when they lie down to rest. We cannot go on cramming forty at a time into a barn; they must have beds—at least, a mattress and a coverlet for two—and they must have room made for them at some fireside, so that they may cook their food. This morning the adjutant-majors started in advance of us, and when we get to Mirebeau, our first halting place, we hope to find our quarters ready for us.

Our Major Viallet had to leave us several days ago. Notwithstanding all his energy, he became incapable at last of getting on his horse, and performing his duties. I fear that he is seriously ill. My faithful friend Fernand de Rougé was in his turn obliged, the day before yesterday, to take the railroad; he was quite worn out. Captain Montécot, who takes Viallet's place, is already in a very low condition, and will not be able to march. We shall then be under the command of Henri Josset, the brave captain of Sourdeval.

Mirebeau, Monday, 20 March, morning

It has been a trying night for the troop; the want of equipments makes them suffer quite as much as before, though they have ten times more room. The people here are surly, and the shopkeepers crafty and cunning, as they are in most places. But, upon the whole, we are in good spirits; we try to drown our sense of sadness by our gaiety. We make good progress. In the middle of the day the heat is oppressive, but the long halt is a very good time with us. The men have cut great sticks to march with. They laugh and chatter all the way, and we often find entertainment in listening to their amusing sayings. The *Marseillaise* has fallen into oblivion, to my great joy. That poor melody has long ceased to be the herald of victory; but it still acts as a powerful incentive to disturbance. Instead of the wild yells of former days, we listen now with great satisfaction to those long plaintive melancholy airs sung by the shepherds on the frontiers of Brittany, and which the Gardes Mobiles of La Manche have at last learned by heart.

And so the day goes by. The road thus far is most uninteresting, and the dust is blinding. Fortunately our marches are now so ordered that we arrive by daylight. If we had better quarters it would not be unendurable.

Mavault, High Road from Loudun to Fontevrault, Tuesday, 21 March, midday

Here we are three leagues, I rejoice to say, from that horrible sepulchre of a place called Loudun. A fatal pestilence is raging there at this moment—the ancient plague, so I am told. If that mysterious scourge ever does appear in these days, it will certainly be in those heaps of filth and rottenness. The inhabitants look as if they belonged to some race of rag-pickers or alchemists of the Middle Ages, carefully preserved through all our revolutions. There, as at Porteau, we had to force our way into the houses; the savages would have left our soldiers in the street. It took me two hours to get my eight men housed, and in consequence of the pestilence, we were not able to leave in the hospital two or three sick men who were no longer able to march.

Turquant-sur-Loire, Wednesday, 22 March, morning

We expected to sleep at Fontevrault; but there was only room for the two battalions of Saint-Lô and Avranches, so that we marched two leagues more yesterday, which gives us two less today. On the road from Fontevrault to Montsoreau we gathered the first leaves of 1871; the elderbushes are already almost green. At four o'clock we left the road, with its borders of walnut-trees, to enter a large town, and at the end of the main street we found ourselves suddenly on the quay. The Loire was rolling majestically at our feet—a dark and rapid stream. It is more than 4,000 metres in breadth at this place, and flows straight towards the west, stretching out a glittering sheet of water for at least two leagues. I had to go half a league farther with my company to reach the village at Turquant, which had been assigned to us. Our Norman lads gazed with curiosity at the artificial caverns hollowed out of the mountain, and on the beautiful white houses by the road-side. We met with a most hospitable reception. The peasants are charming, and their white and red wine seemed to us to be delicious.

After surveying the beautiful valley of Anjou and Touraine from the top of a windmill, which towers 150 feet above the road, I returned to Montsoreau to dinner. The little inn there stands on the edge of the river, exposed to every wind. Whilst our dinner was being prepared, we enjoyed the sight of a magnificent sunset. . . . Spring is already in all its beauty here; the alders and willows by the waterside are putting forth their tender green leaves; everything is returning to life, and warmth, and brightness. . . .

We shall have a three leagues' march along these kindly shores to reach Saumur, where we shall cross the river; this evening we are to sleep at Rosiers, on the road to Angers. The kindness of the people at Turquant is quite affecting. Just now I went into one of the principal houses to inquire after one of my best soldiers, who, after being ill for some days, had for the first time this morning been absent at the roll-call. I found him in a high fever; his hosts had laid him in a comfortable bed, and had made refreshing drinks for him. They begged me to leave him with them. I was only too happy to have found these good Samaritans so opportunely. There is still a great number of them in France, notwithstanding the bad example set by certain provinces.

Angers, Friday, 24 March

I availed myself of the interval of rest we had here to make another expedition to Brissac. I saw my friends again, and had two pleasant days. On reaching Angers this morning, I learnt that we had suddenly come almost to the end of our journey. The station-master had sent word to our colonel that he could transport one battalion through Le Mans, Alençon, Argentan, and Viré, in thirty-six hours. We drew lots, and our battalion won. One detachment starts this evening, and three others tomorrow, one of them under my command. The men will be sent to their homes as soon as they get to Viré. The Colonel returns to La Manche by day's marches with the two other battalions.

My Sub-Lieutenant Mullois has just come back from Paris, where he has been for four days. He escaped with difficulty from the rioters, who are masters of the city. When shall we have reached the lowest depth of the abyss into which France has been sinking for these last eight months?

Captain Montécot has at last been overpowered by fatigue and illness; we have had to leave him behind, and the command had been taken by Henri Josset. The post our comrade has stepped into is not a very hard one, but we all feel that he would have done honour to it, however arduous and severe it might have been.

This evening we shall walk about Angers, we shall dine at the *table d'hôte*, and we shall make as cheerful an ending as we can to this, our last day's march. Yet I thought I should have felt happier than I do, now that all is over.

Viré, Hôtel du Cheval Blanc, Saturday, 25 March, 11 p.m.

Yesterday, at 5 a.m., I left Angers with my detachment, composed of men belonging to the third and fourth companies. I was able to spend an hour at Le Mans, and to make inquiries after my friends.

They have not suffered in person, but their property has been devastated. The château of my cousins De Montesson has been pillaged, and the old house on the Place de l'Éperon has been turned inside out. The doors of the Hôtel de France are riddled with bullets. This poor town, so lately evacuated by the enemy, looked very sad and solitary; three months ago, how animated those streets were—I had almost said how gay! The contrast was deeply affecting.

After a very slow journey, our train brought us to Viré. It had long been dark. We were beginning to rouse ourselves out of the slumbers into which we had fallen on the way, when we found ourselves suddenly in the station-yard, face to face with one another, in the act of parting. I asked myself if I was dreaming. I felt that never had I been so sad as I was at this last moment. I said some few words—I hardly know what; but I besought the men never to allow what they had done or suffered to be lightly spoken of. Their farewells drowned my voice. They let go my hands and those of Léonce, and their brave faces disappeared in the darkness. That was an hour ago; they have all dispersed. We are alone, my lieutenant and I, in a room at the inn. Tomorrow morning we are to start for Mortain, where the colonel will arrive in three days.

We shall hear our bugles no more; they sounded for the last time on the quay of Saumur, at the entrance of the bridge.

EPILOGUE

From La Baronne de Mauni, Folkestone, 1 December 1871

When we received the news that the dreadful retreat on the
Loire was over, and Chanzy's army had arrived at Le Mans, we had
a short breathing time, comparatively free from immediate anxiety.
A host of friends and relations of ours were crowded in that ancient
provinical town, to which we are bound by old family ties, and we
knew that our Roger would be welcomed with kindness on all sides.
Monsieur and Madame de Rougé had hastened to meet our poor
exhausted battalion, and from her we heard the particulars of the
ragged and famished state in which she found those poor boys, whose
letters had always been written so as to keep up our hearts and betray
as little as possible of the dreadful sufferings they had to undergo.
She described them as gaunt and ravenous; but, to her joyful
surprise, she found Roger and Fernand, who had been till then rather
slight and delicate looking, looking much stronger and more stal-
wart than before the war. Their happiness at seeing her had been
great, but my heart was sorely tried on thinking that such a meeting,
qualified as it was by the fears for the future, had not been granted
me. Our kind friends had noticed a passing emotion on my poor
boy's face when he had seen young de Rougé rush to the embrace
of his father and mother. I cried more than once over this phrase.
What would I not have given for those few days in Le Mans and
how hard it seemed at times that the state of my health, and the
anxiety and distress which my venturing on the journey would
cause my invalid husband, obliged me to remain in England!

But we had scarcely had time to realise the short respite, and
already the news of the approach of the Germans in overwhelming
force, and of an inevitable battle, reached us from all sides, and I felt
once more that tight grasp at my heart which one can never forget
after having felt it.

The 12 January we had a letter from my son, dated the 8th,
stating that he could not leave the 'cantonments', because a note had
come from the staff-major, saying that the 21 Corps would perhaps
have to execute a movement that night or on the morrow. Almost
at the same time as this letter the telegram announced a great defeat
of Chanzy close to Le Mans; and the 13th, almost without any

143

preparation, the news came down upon us like a hammerstroke—
Le Mans was in the power of the Germans! Everywhere on those
terrible boards, whose sight I had ere that learnt to shun, the number
of French prisoners, the destruction of our army, were recorded in
large letters. Beaten again! And this time worse than ever! Awful
mistakes, that filled our souls with bitterness, national and provincial
humilation—that soil, where our ancestors had proudly met in
chivalric encounter their loyal English foes, in the power of the
merciless Mecklenburgers—the homes of so many near and dear to
us insulted and ravaged! All that was enough to crush us, but in the
midst of that flood of desolation that swept over us, the sharp cry
from my heart was, 'My son! my son! Where is he? Has his young
life, so much dearer than our own, been made part of the sacrifice?' . . . I cannot express those feelings, nor bear to dwell upon the
agony of that hour. God Almighty alone knows what a supplication
my soul sent forth.

My daughters and myself collected our energies, and, availing
ourselves of the sharpness of the weather, which kept my husband
indoors, and his difficulty in reading English, we succeeded in
keeping from him for twenty-four hours the dreadful fact of the
loss of Le Mans, thus breaking it to him in a manner by degrees.
Moreover, the news had come so suddenly, that if our hopes had
not so often been betrayed, we would have scarcely believed them
to be true. But the next day only brought the terrible confirmation
of our disaster, and we had nothing left but to pray and wait in
blank dismay and misery—that the forthcoming details in the papers
only increased.

Two or three days passed, during which we feared, rather than
hoped, to have any news, as a telegram only could have reached us.
Every ringing of the bell, or loud rap at the door, stopped our
hushed talk, and sent the blood from our faces. None of us could
turn to anything, or dared to express aloud what our thoughts were
full of. Sometimes I looked at the clock, and wondered how long
those cold, cheerless days seemed to be. How many times we
reckoned over and over when we could have news, where the
retreating 21 Corps was likely to be, and the means Madame de
Rougé would be able to take to learn her fate and ours! The bad
weather and the distance from our chapel cut us off from daily
church and the consolation of hearing mass. The newspapers, which
we studied line by line, almost always increased our depression. I

remember reading, in one of the accounts of how the Mobiles were supposed to have suffered in the retreat of Le Mans, that the numerous bodies of slain that strewed the roads and fields had mostly the red trousers of the regular army—and Madame de Rougé had written to me from Le Mans a few days before, how our battalion looked braver, now that red trousers had been given to the men!

A week of suspense seemed long enough, but after that period had elapsed, the uncertainty became almost intolerable. The ever-recurring explanation of letters lost grew to be like an empty sound to my ears; the absence of tidings from all sides seemed a dreadful omen of what might be coming; and then began a trial which I can hardly bear to think of—when, after a long, dreary tearful day, only broken by a few friendly calls of condolence, I had to retire to my room for the night, and think of going to bed, whilst my poor boy might be stretched, wounded and suffering, in the snow, calling for help that did not come, and perhaps thinking of me, afar, and unable to tend him! It seemed beyond the power of endurance. At times I wished to start, without knowing where to go to; I collected a few things, and said I must go; and again the wishes of my husband and the reasoning of friends, who assured me that I would thus miss the news, held me back.

The only events of those days were the hours when the post came in. From our window we saw the postman come from a long distance. After a time I knew all his habits and movements, and as he came nearer and nearer to our house, we felt suffocating with the thought, 'What did he bring?' When he had passed our door, a sickening shock of disappointment came over us. I think the man grew to be aware of our feelings, by seeing constantly our mournful, anxious faces at the window, watching him coming into the square, and he seemed to turn his head away when he had to pass our door without anything for us.

At last one day, the 13th of that purgatory, there was one letter with the well-known blue stamp. Madame de Rougé's writing— not his! The minute that elapsed in opening it was dreadful. Her short, hurried epistle was a gleam of hope, but not more. Both our children had been seen, living and unwounded, on the morning of the 19th; but we knew by the papers that the 21 Corps had been engaged that very day. It had been a Sunday. Oh, how we had prayed on that Sunday! I think no one can feel the meaning of the *Kyrie Eleison* who has not heard it and repeated it in such an immense disaster as ours, when a whole nation, feeling out of reach of human help, and as if the earth was giving way under it, cries to heaven for mercy.

Two days after the letter of our friend had reached us, there was a loud knock at the door, and, for the first time, an exclamation of joy on the stairs. There was a whole bundle of letters! Three from our own dear Roger, who, as usual had written to us from every place where it was possible. He was safe, he had distinguished himself, and the sense of having done his duty had cheered his spirits. What a renewal of happiness! What deep thanksgiving! Then and then only we felt how much the long strain had taxed our strength.

From La Baronne de Mauni, Folkestone, 12 December 1871

Time had passed, however, slowly and sadly, and in the square, where we had watched the falling leaves of 1870 and the long winter's snow, the trees were green again, and our weary hearts were still vainly craving for the return of our young 'Mobile'. The armistice was over, peace was signed, and they were farther than ever from their Norman homes. Though the hourly dangers of the war were past, there was much to fear; and depressed by the continued suspense, our minds dwelt on the protracted fatigue of their marches; and when we were hoping every day to hear that they had begun to turn their steps homeward, the news of the revolution in Paris, where troops that could be relied on would be so much wanted, renewed our apprehension. Again the communications threatened to be interrupted, and, although we had heard that the Garde Mobile had been disarmed, our sense of relief was not complete, and we reckoned again and again how and when our dear Roger could return to us. Our calculations had led us to hope that about 3 April we might see him. From that date we began to go and meet the boat. How wildly our hearts beat when the steamer came in sight! How we watched every figure as it emerged from the steps! The last passed—he was not there, and we had another day and night of feverish expectation. Day after day we went there for a whole week, each disappointment increasing our anxiety. On Friday, the 7th, we had calculated that, taking into account every possible delay, he must be there. The boat came—a young man was on board looking eagerly towards the landing-place, and wearing a military cloak. It was a stranger! Our hearts sank within us. Again and again I asked if there was no one still on board, and, as the last hope vanished, I felt sick and faint with the bitter disappointment. Was it then as I feared even without daring to contemplate it? Had our poor boy been called away to that dreadful civil war, and had I missed even the consolation of looking at him again? Such a feeling of anguish went through my heart as I can hardly bear to think of. Some ladies who had come to see the arrival of the boat came up to me with words of sympathy and kindness, which I scarcely heard or understood. I tried to thank them, and walked away. I believe the deep feeling of misery I experienced must have been depicted on my face, for one of these ladies, whom I met again the next day, said the sight of it had haunted her fancy so that she could not sleep for the whole night.

Only two of us found strength to go to the boat on that next day, and were rewarded with that first glimpse that I felt no physical fatigue could have made me give up. There he was at last! Of course the change was very great, but every feeling was merged in the joy and thanksgiving of our hearts on beholding him again. These emotions were too deep for expression. Those hours in which his words, his changed aspect and manner, made us first realise what had been the struggle of a nation who had fought and suffered almost to death, those are moments never to be forgotten, no more than the Mass on Easter Sunday, when he came in his worn, battle-stained uniform and knelt with us in the place where we had prayed and wept—oh, with what heartrending anguish!—whilst he was fighting far away.

In another church, in a village in France, there is now a marble slab put up in thanksgiving for that return. The old blacksmith (a veteran from other wars), the carpenter's lads, and other humble friends, whose homely, affectionate farewells followed him when he went forth, will be the better for remembering, every time they see it, how Almighty God's protection carried him safe through it all.

Select Bibliography

CHANZY, GENERAL. *La Deuxième Armée de la Loire*. Paris, 1873.

FAVRE, JULES. Government of the National Defence. Tr. H. Clark. London, 1873.

FREYCINET, CHARLES DE. *La Guerre en Province, pendant le siège de Paris*. Paris, 1872.

HOWARD, MICHAEL. *The Franco-Prussian War*. London, 1961.

Journals of Field Marshal Count von Blumenthal. Tr. Major A. D. Gillespie-Addison. London, 1903.

MOLTKE, FIELD MARSHAL COUNT HELMUT VON. *The Franco-German War of 1870–71*. Tr. Archibald Forbes. London, 1907.

POURCET, GENERAL. *Campagne sur la Loire*. Paris, 1874.

Index